To Stanley

The reyeode

OF

Bill Pamily

(and Jun Rapp)

originally published by your old friend
in 1959   Jay Marshall

and now by you-know-who
in 1891
            David Meyer

MW00512684

THE
LIFE AND TIMES
OF
AUGUSTUS RAPP

THE
SMALL TOWN
SHOWMAN

With sincere good wishes   Augustus Rapp

THE
LIFE AND TIMES
OF
AUGUSTUS RAPP

THE
SMALL TOWN
SHOWMAN

Written by Himself

With an Introduction by
Robert Parrish

And a Foreword by
Dr. Joseph French
Performing Arts Department
Henry Ford Museum and Greenfield Village

David Meyer ✺ Magic Books
Glenwood, Illinois

Copyright 1959 © by Augustus Rapp. Copyright
renewed 1987 by Jay Marshall, publisher of
the first, limited edition. This edition,
extensively reorganized and edited by
Marcia Boggs, copyright © 1991 by Meyerbooks,
Publisher. All rights reserved. No part of
this book may be reproduced in any form or by
any means, electronic or mechanical, including
photocopy, recording or any information retrival
system, without permission in writing from
Meyerbooks, Publisher.
Text typeset in New Century Schoolbook
by Francis D. Heitler

[Hardcover]   ISBN 0-916638-44-8
[Softcover]   ISBN 0-916638-45-6

Library of Congress Cataloging-in-Publication Data

Rapp, Augustus, 1871–1961.
    The life and times of Augustus Rapp, the small town showman /
written by himself ; with an introduction by Robert Parrish ;
foreword by Joseph French.
      p.   cm.
  ISBN 0-916638-44-8
  1. Rapp, Augustus, 1871-1961. 2. Magicians--United States-
-Biography. 3. Entertainers--United States--Biography.
4. Conjuring--United States. I. Title.
GV1545.R35A3 1990
793.8--dc20
[B]   90-30694
                                                               CIP

Meyerbooks, Publisher
235 West Main Street
Glenwood, Illinois 60425

CONTENTS

ILLUSTRATIONS

Photographs are courtesy of the American Museum of Magic

FOREWORD

Henry Ford felt that the invention of the automobile changed the way we lived to such an extent that the world he grew up in was vanishing forever. Even after a mere eighty years, a world without rapid means of transportation is difficult to imagine. Difficult, but not impossible. The affection we feel for what must have been a more romantic era has prompted a widespread nostalgia for the nineteenth century in general, and for the 1890s in particular.

It was not the automobile alone that shook the world. It was not even mainly the automobile. The technological advances that brought a sudden end to the way American life was lived at the turn of the century was not in the automotive field, but in the field of entertainment.

I do not believe I really comprehended the changes that were prompted by the successive sweeps throughout culture and our lives by the advent of talking pictures in the thirties and television in the fifties, until I read **The Life and Times of Augustus Rapp, The Small Town Showman.** Until we were enlightened by the flickering images on a screen, we really believed that our values and our goals were the same as those of the people in the next block, the next town, the next county, the next state. Until we actually saw ourselves and our neighbors, both near and far, with our own eyes, the great distances that the automobile seemed to diminish retained their original breadth.

As we tour through the Midwest with Gus Rapp, we discover a forgotten world. We see the small towns of America from about 1891 to 1941. It is not a particularly clean or pleasant world but it is a fascinating one.

The towns once visited by Gus Rapp, by medicine shows, by circuses, and by actors like the Joseph Jeffersons have been cleaned up, sanitized, and homogenized. In attempting to live up to their own television image, they have acquired a sameness. Developers have moved in to construct shopping malls with eight movie theaters and rental headquarters for video cassettes. The same level of entertainment is now available to everyone. A level that is technologically higher than ever before but weaker in some respects in performance skills.

Performers rarely have the opportunity now to develop and hone their skills to perfection in even one area of show business, yet here is a man who could entertain an audience for an entire week; who could provide six full evenings of entertainment without ever repeating a trick or an act; and, most importantly, do it without ever boring the audience. Gus Rapp was a magician, a juggler, a mentalist, a comedian, an actor, a ventriloquist, a puppeteer — he was anything he desired to be, anything the show needed that night. He was a showman!

Dr. Joseph French
Performing Arts Dept.
Henry Ford Museum
& Greenfield Village
Dearborn, Michigan

INTRODUCTION

It appears that there have always been roving showmen: minstrels, mountebanks, traveling players. Being such a trouper is a bit different from being an actor, or performing artist per se. You are not booked, your coming is not arranged for. You do not depend upon any of the machinery that makes the showman an organization man. You just take to the road and keep moving.

Such showmen differ from pure vagabonds in that they have a calling: to perform. This distinguishes them from the great American character the Confidence Man, although the Confidence Man (as in Huck Finn) is often a sham showman, and the showman practically has to have a bit of the con artist in his make-up in order to survive. The conditions for doing this sort of thing have become increasingly difficult to find. A widespread population endowed with leisure, loneliness and a capacity for wonderment is required. Even in the 1890s when Gus Rapp first set out with a magic show, the proper field for the truly independent showman was not visible to the untrained eye. The small Midwestern towns of that golden era were already pretty self-sufficient and sophisticated social units. It wasn't hard to get the theater dates, but without the made-up glamor of a reputation, your show didn't attract enough of the citizens to turn a profit. Too many had something else to do when the sun went down, had places to congregate and had learned that wonderment was only for children.

Someone had to point out to Gus that beyond the outskirts of these communities lay a network of unnamed crossroads settlements where civilization was but dimly felt, a hinterland where a fellow still could make a buck and remain his own master. Rapp disappeared across the fresh fields as completely as though he had followed his friend Carl Ackley into uncharted Africa. He remained lost for 50 years. His route did not appear in the columns of *The Sphinx* or the theatrical papers. Aside from a few friends, no one in the business ever heard of him. Yet there he was, moving with his little caravan across the lovely hills and meadows of the dairy country, through the byways of the corn belt and the wildernesses of the rural south.

The writer of this introduction has lived in a village of 500 souls in the wilds of Iowa and sat entranced in the tent show, delighted by the Toby sketch, the sentimental songs, everything. He has also sat in Percy Abbott's old circus tent at Colon, Michigan, and seen an hour of magic that he will never forget, performed by Gus Rapp. In short, he has been a privileged individual, and is happy to pass along to the reader the privilege of glimpsing an all but forgotten world and an almost lost art, the world and art of Gus Rapp. Rapp was a wonderful magician and a delightful performer. His repertoire consisted of the old time classics. Once you have seen these tricks performed by masters, it is pretty hard to find anything else that will stand up in comparison. It isn't just that they have an antique charm. As another aged gentleman named Gus once said to me, "If Kellar used a trick, you could be pretty sure it was a good trick." These tricks all had the elements that magic should have. The old-timers who became masters had a sense of how much you had to put into these tricks in order to reveal their greatness. Kellar writes of how long he worked on the Growth of Flowers, while an employee of the Fakir of Ava, before the Fakir would put his stamp of approval upon the presentation. Rapp comments that after performing steadily for five years, he felt that he was beginning to do his tricks in a satisfactory manner. After fifty years he could say with confidence that he had a good show, but he made no claim to being a great magician.

Well, I can say that he was pretty great. He was the first man I ever saw roll a paper cornucopia for the DeKolta flower trick with a single graceful movement of the hands. I suppose the other masters did this also. But that is the touch that makes the trick. He also had a personal hold that sprang from

[xiv]

his sense of self, the hidden message that is the reason for performance. Since this is almost impossible to describe, we have few records that are very helpful in pinning down the essential characteristics of any performer. I can't be very helpful on this score, either, but can only mention one's immediate sense in Rapp's presence of the shrewd yet somehow guileless face and an apparently constitutional optimism.

The rural slums in which Gus played for so many years are disappearing or have turned into real estate subdivisions. The only thing he liked about them was the fact that they gave him an audience. He wasn't a man of the soil and he didn't share the farmer's easy acceptance of all the processes of nature. As a matter of fact, he had an acutely discriminating sense of smell. But in spite of the hardships he endured, it was a wonderful life. He loved nature and the out-of-doors. He loved his work. And he was a really independent man. No matter what, there was always another little town just ahead.

Robert Parrish

THE
LIFE AND TIMES
OF
AUGUSTUS RAPP

THE
SMALL TOWN
SHOWMAN

CHAPTER ONE

A SHORT HISTORY OF GUS RAPP

I was born dead. At least that was the decision of the Negro midwife who officiated at the, to me, important natal ceremony. There was no need for a doctor who charged as high as five dollars for such services. Anyone could tie a string around the umbilical cord, cut it with a pair of dirty scissors, and not charge anything for doing it. After the midwife had completed her bit of amateur surgery, she started to prepare me for burial. Undertakers hadn't come into existence. While working on me another old Negro woman came in to view the remains. At first sight she decided I wasn't "daid." She insisted that they immerse me in warm water. It was cold weather. In a short time one eyelid flickered a little, then the other moved a little, and I wasn't "daid" at all. Present day procedure would have been to rush me to a hospital for treatment. They couldn't do this at the time as there was no hospital and transportation was of the slow horse and buggy type that was not capable of being rushed. The old woman who discovered that I was alive must have taken good care of me, as I have nearly ninety years to tell the tale. With two dark-skinned women as my first benefactors I ought to claim African ancestry.

This precarious opening page of my life took place in Jeffersonville, Indiana on January 29th, 1871. My father was born in West Point, New York. His name was Anthony Rapp. My mother was born in Philadelphia. Her name was Mary Roemer. Although christened Francis Augustine Rapp, I always used the name Augustus.

1

Jeffersonville was founded in 1802 according to the plans of Thomas Jefferson. The city never could boast of having many industries. Over the years it had a State Reformatory, which later became a soap factory. It had the Army Quartermaster's Supply Depot and a shipyard. In recent years it had become noted as a marriage center. Kentucky marriage laws were strict, while those of Indiana were not. Kentucky couples wishing to be married would cross the river bridge by way of street car and could be married at once. One street was devoted to marriage and the buildings had large signs such as "Marriage Parlor," "Justice of the Peace, Reverend P. K. Potts," etc. Each marriage parlor furnished witnesses. Some had solicitors who would grab the couples and steer them to their places of business.

I am told that I was born on the bank of the Ohio River. Do not misunderstand me; I do not mean that I was born at the water's edge, among the mud, gravel, clam shells, and dead catfish. I mean that the house I was born in was situated on the bank of the beautiful Ohio. The Ohio is beautiful only when it is not flooded and muddy, and at places where the cities do not empty their unbeautiful refuse and garbage into it.

The house in which I was born was situated 100 feet from the water's edge, but only a few feet higher than water level. When the lovely Ohio flooded, we had two feet of water in our house. We overcame this accustomed situation by moving upstairs. The cellar rats must have had the same experience, because they moved with us. Food was scarce. The attic housed about 200 pigeons. When the rats needed food they pillaged the nest and ate the young pigeons. When my parents needed food they ate the older pigeons. The pigeons were able to fly to dry land and forage for themselves. When the flood receded, we moved downstairs. So did the rats. The pigeons returned to their normal way of living, which consisted mainly of eating and defacing the roof and interior of the attic in a manner not approved of by present day health authorities. All this happened before I was born, or before I was old enough to appreciate the beauties of life.

2

Pa went fishing the day I was born, and when he didn't come home for a long time Ma commenced wishing I was old enough to be sent to the corner saloon to see if he was loafing there, which he probably was. When he finally came home, without any fish, he took one look at me and said, "I wish to goodness I'd been to home, then this wouldn't a-happened. It looks like it's going to be a cripple or an idiot because it has flat feet, weak ribs, and its head runs to a peak like a cokeenut. What is it anyway, a boy or a girl?" Ma said, "I don't know yet, because it just came and I haint had time to look." "Well," said Pa, "It looks to me like a great big angle worm. You'd better put it on a hook and line and throw it in the river, you might ketch sumpin' worth while." Ma, being the contrary animal she was, would not do anything Pa told her to do, so she did not throw me in the river. Later on, when I wanted to know where I came from, Ma said she paid the doctor ten dollars for bringing me. I thought that was too much, because a bird brought the folks next door a baby free of charge.

My life was handicapped from the start. I did not inherit any genes of value from my parents, as Pa worked on a river boat which bootlegged whiskey and Ma slung hash in a cheap restaurant. At least I came from respectable parents. I was born a nudist and a pauper. There was no silver spoon in my mouth; I didn't even have teeth. I didn't have a shirt on my back, and my chest was in the same predicament. I didn't know anything and couldn't write my own name. Like a hen I had to start from scratch, and that's just what I did, because they told me I had the itch. The best that could be said of me was that I was a thing that bellowed at one end and suffered with juvenile delinquency at the other end. If birth control had been in style at that time they might have done a better job on me. I was so poor that my first belongings had to be donated to me. They were a three cornered piece of cloth, some corn starch powder and a quart of milk. Not the kind of milk that comes in cans and has to be adulterated with water; it was real milk from unvaccinated and discontented cows. If any water was added, it was done by the milkman before he sold it.

3

In spite of the mismanagement of the first few weeks of my life I continued to improve until I developed into a reasonable facsimile of a small human being. Even though the midwife did not charge too much for bringing me I must have been worth it, because I lasted from the tallow candle to the neon light period and I am not burned out.

I never did find out how I happened to be named Francis Augustus. My guess is that they thought if I developed into a good boy, they would use the name Francis because St. Francis was a good and holy man; and if I turned out to be a bad boy, they would use the name Augustus because Augustus was a heathen emperor. It seems I became a bad boy. I wish they had named me Adeline then I could have been a girl. Nobody would have known the difference but me, unless I told them. Also, I would have had a song named after me.

As soon as I was old enough to do it, I acquired every known childhood disease. I had measles, scarlet fever, whooping cough. The only ailments that missed me were fallen arches and gout. At the age of five, just about the time I had recovered from all of these pathological conditions, my mother died, leaving my father with four small children. All that I can remember of her is kissing her on the forehead before the casket was closed. She was buried in Hartford, Wisconsin.

Our home was broken and my father was unable to establish another. The children were separated and went to live with strangers. I, who was destined to be a migratory animal, lived with more neighbors, aunts, uncles, grandmothers, friends, and enemies, than I thought it possible for one little boy to have. One family would harbor me until they could endure me no longer and then inflict me on some other unsuspecting persons. I was far from being a nice little boy. My sweet face and long golden curls were not in harmony with my mischievous disposition. My guess is that I changed homes so often because I made life miserable for my generous benefactors. Perhaps that was why I had to endure a year's imprisonment in an orphanage, sentenced there by an aunt who did not like me on account of my prankish tendencies.

4

Here is a sample or two. My uncle had a cigar factory. During the noon hour I played with the counting apparatus of a threshing machine and made it register about fifty bushels more of grain than had been threshed. At another time I was playing along side of a mill race with a girl cousin of my own age. There was a rubbish pile nearby. On it was an old-fashioned metal bath tub which was rusty and leaky. As it somewhat resembled a boat, I thought it would be nice if I gave my cousin a boat ride. We managed to drag the tub out and put it in the water. As soon as we got into the tub, it upset, spilling us into the water. A passing man rescued us from drowning. He also reported the incident to my aunt and what she did to me I don't like to place on record.

If that man hadn't come along just when he did, I wouldn't be able to tell the story and my aunt wouldn't have done what she did. Besides what she did, she was the leader of the gangsters who conspired to put me in the orphanage. This house of refuge didn't suit me at all. The good sisters who conducted this penal institution were strict disciplinarians. I was forced to be a good little boy, and of course I didn't like that. I had to say my prayers before meals, after meals, before retiring, after arising, and on other occasions. What boy likes to pray? Meals were not as good as those my aunt furnished me. Also, some of the boys suffered with ringworm which had to be treated with acetic acid, and I was appointed to the position of chief medicine man. I had some vinegar in a tin cup and a sponge with which to apply it. The boys filed past me and I would apply the vinegar to the diseased parts. I didn't like the job, as I thought the disease might be contagious and I might acquire it. I was suspicious that the tin cup containing the vinegar was also used to serve coffee at meals. I was also delegated to read aloud selections from a book entitled *Lives of Saints*. I did this while the other boys were eating. I never found out whether this procedure was intended to increase or diminish the boy's appetites. I do know that it put me nearly an hour late for my dinner, which wasn't conducive to my acquiring a happy disposition, especially in view of the fact that I was always hungry.

Some of the boys had lice, which fact didn't help any to my enjoyment of my foster home. A wholesale grocer had a barrel of burnt molasses which was unsalable. Not knowing of any method to dispose of it profitably, he decided to present it to the orphanage, a very generous and charitable act. The children used it on bread instead of butter.

The institution boasted of a sickroom for the boys when they were ill or injured. Here they were given special attention and, of course, did not have to attend school. With my healthy constitution I knew that I would never be sent to the infirmary on account of illness, so I decided to get there without being sick. I made up my mind to acquire a bad case of rheumatism. I told the sister I had a severe pain in my leg, so bad that I had to walk with a limp. At that time, about 1881, all body pains were called rheumatism. As my pain had no visible evidence of its existence excepting the limp, the sister believed me and sent me to the sickroom. Of course I had to remain in bed, but this was compensated for by the fact that I had good meals and that I didn't have to attend school at this time.

The nursing sister tied a girdle of strung horse chestnuts around my midriff. This was an old fashioned remedy for rheumatic pains. It did not prove to be of benefit in my case. I continued to suffer and to limp. Once a week a doctor came from the city to attend the sick boys. He prescribed some pills for me. When he came a week later I still had the pains and the limp. The doctor seemed puzzled. He gave me one pill. When he came back after an hour I was still suffering severely, but the doctor was no longer perplexed. He knew I had been cheating. He had given me a morphine pill, potent enough to kill any pain. This the sister told me later. When I still complained of the ache he prescribed another treatment calculated to make me lose the pain in a hurry. It was a poultice composed of some drastic irritating substance to be applied to the leg. The sister did this and the next morning my leg was blistered from my hip to my ankle. I had now acquired a real pain and a real limp. I was glad to announce that my rheumatic pains and limp were gone. Also I was glad to go back to the classroom and inferior meals.

My brain was continually working overtime trying to think of something I might do which would cause me to be expelled from the orphanage. I decided I would pretend I was insane so they would transfer me to an insane asylum. Behind the orphanage there was a marsh which was frozen solid in winter. I arose early one morning and went out on the marsh, holding a long stick with an inverted tin gallon measure on its upper end. I jumped and scampered around and uttered peculiar noises. This was my idea of the way a crazy person might act. It was winter and I was nearly dead with cold before a watchful sister finally discovered me and took me into the building. Breakfast was over and I did not have any food until noon. They did not send me to the sickroom, nor to the insane asylum. Instead they sent for my aunt to come and take me away. The sisters didn't want me and my aunt didn't want me, but I had to live with her until someone else would take me and support me. Truly, I was a boy without a country.

After attending about twenty schools I graduated at the age of eighteen from the eighth grade. This shoved me out into the big, cold, cruel, bitter world to fight my battles alone, as my father had died. So far I had been able to keep out of the reform school and I wasn't a bit frightened. I had to be a self made man, and subsequent events have shown that I wasn't very successful. If I had been older I might have acquired a wife who would have gladly assumed the responsibility. In which case I wouldn't be what I am, and this story would never have been written.

As soon as I was out of school, I secured a position with a wholesale dry goods and notion house. This work didn't suit me at all. I was too confined. I wanted out of doors work. Being inside of a poorly ventilated building and inhaling the odors which came from calico, gingham, and other dyed fabrics gave me the idea that I might develop a case of consumption (now called tuberculosis). My mother died of that dread disease and I was warned against it. An uncle wanted me to work for him and learn goldsmithing. This, too, was indoor work. I had been associated with aunts and uncles for so long that I wanted other associations. They wanted to dominate me, and being of Dutch extraction I was too stubborn to allow them to do so. I thought there was no future for me in the dry goods business and it seems I was right, because now, sixty years later, the business is out. The firm went bankrupt and every person connected with the affair is dead.

I remained five years and used my spare time, evenings, and Saturdays trying to find a more desirable occupation. From the uncle who had a cigar factory I learned to make cigars in molds according to the manner of that time. I learned photography. I studied optometry (it was called peddling spectacles at that time). I worked nights at Vizay's Dancing Academy, as instructor, in another of my attempts to get into a business where I could get rich without much work. I also took lessons in taxidermy from Carl E. Akely, who later became a noted taxidermist and African explorer. I thought I would like to be a naturalist and collected and preserved many natural history specimens, including thousands of butterflies. I also studied legerdemain, or magic, as it is more commonly called. This was the only endeavor in which I was successful. Magical exhibitions always fascinated me, especially when I didn't understand the methods used in producing some really remarkable effects.

Nothing of interest happened at either the store or dancing academy, but plenty happened at the taxidermy shop. Mr. Akely was the leader in his art at that time because he had revolutionized the method of preserving animals. Heretofore they had been stuffed, which meant that the skin had been sewed onto a bag and then stuffed with cotton or a similar soft material. Iron rods were used to take the place of legs and backbone. I never saw a stuffed animal that had a true, lifelike appearance. The improved method consisted of making a solid model of the body of the animal and mounting the skin on it. To do this, one had to be both an artist and a sculptor. At the present time this method is in general use. All

8

preserved animals are mounted, not stuffed. This man taught me the art of taxidermy and also allowed me to store my magical outfit in his building. He permitted me to use his tools and material for constructing anything I needed for my show. Carl was one of the best friends I had at that time.

I liked to study all branches of natural history, anything that had "ology" at the end of its name. Especially, I liked ornithology and oology, the sciences pertaining to birds and eggs. Yes, I robbed bird's nests. It was a common custom. One could obtain books from the public library, telling how to do it. There were egg collectors' clubs, members of which would trade eggs in the same manner that postage stamps are traded today. This was a cruel and barbarous practice. There were many barbarians running loose in those days. I tried to justify my actions by making myself believe that I was a naturalist doing scientific work. If there was anything scientific about me, no one was able to tell where I kept it but myself. Neither did anyone know that I was an osteologist just because I had a collection of bones. Bones of the lower animals did not satisfy me; I wanted human bones. I not only wanted them, I got them. From a student at the medical college I obtained the head and hand of a woman who had committed suicide. The skull had been trepanned, which means that a circular piece had been cut from the top of it so the brain could be removed for study and examination. I articulated the hand and wrist bones and I had two fairly good osteological specimens.

Next I discovered an old and abandoned cemetery. It had not been used for burial purposes for over forty years. Originally it had been outside of the city, but after extension of the city limit several times, the piece of ground became part of the city proper. In order to make it level for building purposes, part of it had been graded by removing five feet of earth. This brought what was left of the remains of the buried bodies about one foot below the surface. Heavy rains and the like had worn gullies in the soil, exposing rotted coffins and bones. I collected a bountiful supply of bones from this mine of osteological treasures. I had to sneak them into my room at the place where I was living. In a short time I had a pile of leg and arm bones, ribs, vertebrae, etc. While the heap was small I could keep it covered with old clothing, and so hide it from view. It finally became so large that I could not keep it concealed any longer. When the women of the family with which I was living discovered the gruesome remains, they were scared stiff. I was ordered to remove my precious specimens instantly, which I did. Not knowing what to do with them, I took the larger ones back to the graveyard. The smaller ones, like those of the fingers and toes, I dropped through the grating of a city sewer. I have often wondered how all these parts of the body are going to assemble themselves on resurrection day. The skull with the top cut off I sold to a man who wanted to use it for a holder for pipes and tobacco. So ended my career as an osteologist. The money I received for the skull I used to pay for a butterfly net, which was the start of my becoming an entomologist who specialized in lepidoptera.

When the archeology bug bit me, I decided to open an Indian mound on a farm a few miles from the city. I obtained permission to dig into it and induced Carl to go along to help. We had no horse and buggy, so the only way to get to the farm was to walk. We not only walked, but we also carried picks, shovels, and a box for our finds. It was a hot day in July. We arrived at the farm at noon, nearly exhausted.We nevertheless dug most of the afternoon. We did not get anything, though, except overworked and overheated. The ground was solid, and the aborigine who was planted there must have been put to stay. Toward evening, we decided to quit and return on the next Saturday to finish digging. We left and did not notify the farmer we were going to return. The next Saturday we repeated the long tramp under another hot sun. When we arrived at our one-grave cemetery, we were greeted with a real surprise. The hole had been filled. A calf had died during the week and the farmer had used the ready-made grave to bury it. Later, someone told me that the rise in the ground was not an Indian mound but an elevation caused by a load of earth someone had dumped there some years earlier and before the farmer had lived there. Carl lost interest in my scientific expeditions, and I was cured of my desire to be an archeologist.

We enjoyed ourselves at the taxidermy shop because Carl appreciated fun and humor. He liked anything that would cause a laugh. The shop had an odor worse than any slaughtering house. We who worked in it had become accustomed to it and did not notice it, but a sensitive outsider would nearly faint. Customers visiting the shop were mostly a refined group of people and were not used to such an odor. It was Carl's delight to keep a woman there for as long as he could, just to watch her reaction. When she was about ready to collapse, he would open the door and allow pure air to enter.

His pet vexation was the woman with the dead canary to be mounted. Women would come to the shop with tears in their eyes, a woebegone look on their faces, and a dead canary wrapped in a handkerchief. The way they moaned and groaned would lead one to think the bird was a near and dear relative. The bird must be mounted in a life-like manner, as he was to occupy a place in her room where she could gaze on him before retiring, feel bad, and perhaps even offer a prayer. They would depart, still weeping, with the information that the bird would be ready for delivery in two weeks. Most women never returned for their darling birdie. In a few days they would cease mourning and discover a bird store stocked with canaries, one of which could be purchased for less money than it cost to mount the dead one. When the mounting was not paid for in advance, Carl was the loser, as there was no sale for mounted canaries even though the birds were the perfection of the taxidermal art. After he had accumulated about fifteen such liabilities, he had to devise a means for disposing of them.

He developed an excellent scheme. When persons, usually women, brought a canary to be mounted, he would tell them the bird would be ready for delivery in two weeks and ask for payment in advance. As all canaries are similar in appearance, he would select one of those already mounted and deliver it to the customer when she called for her bird. The dead canary was thrown in the stove and cremated, and no one ever questioned the authenticity of the bird. In this manner he disposed of all of his feathered liabilities.

As there was no public garbage collection in the city at that time, the bodies of skinned animals had to be disposed of in some other way. Small bodies, like those of birds, could be cremated in the heating stove. Larger bodies were not disposed of so easy. To get rid of the body of a large eagle, we wrapped it in a large sheet of paper. While crossing a bridge at night, I dropped the bundle into the river which flowed through the city. In a few days, after the body had decayed, the police were dragging the river for the body of a drowned man. Their grappling hook brought up the bundled eagle. Not being experienced in human anatomy, they thought it to be the body of an infant and so informed the reporters. The daily papers made a news item out of the occurrence. As we heard no more about the matter, I presume that when the proper persons examined the body they discovered the mistake.

Getting rid of so large an object as a skinned horse head and neck was a different problem. I was not able to carry that to the river under cover of darkness. We dug a hole and buried it in our backyard. Someone looking out of an upstairs window saw what we were doing and reported the facts to the police. We received notice from the authorities to exhume the offending object and remove it from the city. Which we did.

Carl was an epicure, that is if one can stretch his imagination sufficiently to make himself believe that an eater of snakes is such a person. Carl ate some of the flesh of every kind of animal that came into the shop, provided it had not started to decay. He sampled alligator, snake, dog, owl, and other meats supposedly unfit for human food. On one occasion he neatly cut up the body of a cat. He took it to the woman he boarded with, told her it was rabbit, and asked her to fry it. None who ate it discovered the deception, but when Carl told them it was cat meat several persons became nauseated. Also, the landlady hinted that she would be pleased if Carl found another boarding place, which he didn't.

Occasionally Carl made artificial curiosities for show or exhibition purposes. He took the upper half of a monkey and the rear half of a large fish, joined them, and made a mermaid. It did not have the lovely countenance of the fabled mermaid in pictures, but the whole affair seemed to be a million years old. It was sufficiently realistic so that spectators at fair and carnival shows would gaze at it with wonder and amazement. Carl also had another idea in mind. He wanted to construct a monstrous sea serpent, to be secretly placed on an ocean beach to be discovered by someone. The presumption would be that it was washed on shore by the waves. The discoverer would undoubtedly be Carl. He intended to make the body of a framework covered with papier mache to give it the proper shape. This would be covered with scales from some large fish, like those of a tarpon. These scales were to be graduated according to size, being large at the neck and small near the tail. The tail was to be made of flat seashells ground smaller so as not to be recognized as such. The head was to be made of papier mache decorated with whiskers of horsetail hair. The whole affair was to be highly colored. Carl never found time to transform this idea into a reality. He did find time, however, to engage in other deceptive practices.

A large circus elephant died, and as a circus had no use for a dead elephant, it was offered for sale at a cheap price. Carl bought the elephant. He had to go to the circus winter headquarters to skin it when the temperature was below zero. The elephant was in a cold barn. With the aid of an assistant Carl tackled the job. Before leaving home, he had prepared some articles for use in practicing his tricks. An old watch, a piece of watch chain, a safety pin, a few copper coins, etc. were dipped into molten paraffin which had been colored green. This gave the articles a shiny, greenish look. Reporters from large city newspapers were on hand to watch the proceedings. It was too cold for them to remain in the barn for any great length of time, so they stayed in the warm office and made periodic visits to the barn to see how the work was progressing. After the elephant had been disemboweled and while the

13

newspaper men were absent, Carl cut a small slit in the animal's stomach and inserted the prepared articles. The next time the reporters were on the scene, Carl decided it was time to examine the beast's stomach. Of course, he cut into it on the side opposite the small slit and found the prepared articles. Carl explained they had been turned green by the digestive juices. One of the circus men knew just when the elephant had swallowed the watch — it was the time he ate someone's vest. The reporters made a lengthy news item out of this, and the story was published in all of the nation's leading dailies. This furnished plenty of amusement for Carl and his associates.

Carl brought the skin and skeleton home. He placed the skin in a liquid preservative until he could find a profitable sale for it. There was no immediate demand for elephant skins; and by the time a museum of natural history was in the market for one the epidermis had slipped, thus rendering it unfit to be used for scientific purposes. He finally sold the skin for a small sum to a maker of leather goods, who had it tanned and made into expensive pocketbooks and handbags. He was the only person who made any money out of that dead elephant.

Carl has quit fooling people.* He has quit everything. He made several expeditions into what he termed "Brightest Africa," going there in quest of big game. During one of these expeditions, he contracted a fever and died. He is buried in a jungle of equatorial Africa.

At the time when I was working with Carl, the city in which I lived had a dime museum which, besides exhibiting a motley array of mounted birds and other curiosities, had some platform attractions. Occasionally one of these was a magician. He would do a few minor tricks and sell a small book for ten cents which explained how the tricks were done. He

---

*Carl was Carl Ethan Akeley, 1864-1926. He was a famous American naturalist and animal sculpture artist. After leaving Milwaukee in 1895, Carl went to the Field Museum in Chicago, where he became famous for the Akeley method of mounting habitat groups. The method depends on sculpture, modeling and a thorough knowledge of anatomy. In 1923 he wrote his best known book, *In Brightest Africa.*

worked only a few minutes every hour and the rest of the time sat on a chair on the platform and flirted with the girl patrons in the hall. This seemed like a fortune when the ordinary worker was paid only one dollar a day for twelve hours of hard work. This started me thinking and the outcome of my thoughts was that I would like to be a magician, get some of that easy money and have plenty of opportunity to flirt with the girls.

I didn't know just how to get started. When I was a small boy I had a cheap paper-covered book about magical secrets. It told of a trick in which the hand was shown empty, then closed, and then opened with a piece of money in it. The money was concealed in the sleeve and secretly slipped into the hand at the proper time. This seemed easy and I decided to fool my grandmother. I didn't have any money so I used a charred match. Grandma wasn't very much impressed with my trick. She said the match came out of my sleeve.

At Litt's Museum I purchased the ten cent book on magic. It didn't tell much of anything, but it aroused my curiosity about the mystic art. I practiced a few easy tricks, thinking that would be a step in the right direction. So at the public library I discovered a copy of *Modern Magic* by Professor Hoffmann. This book told everything there was to be known about magic at that time. Then along came the noted magician of the day, Alexander Herrmann, who gave an elaborate two-hour show at high prices in the best theatre in the city. I saw his show every night for a week and the theatre was filled to capacity every night. I estimated his receipts must have been $2,000 or perhaps more a night. Immediately I lost interest in the cheap $100 a week museum platform performer. His pay looked like small potatoes. I now wanted a big show like Herrmann's, and as I knew the secrets of all of his magic it wasn't hard for me to convince myself that I could give as good a show as he did because I could do all the things he did. Why couldn't I be a noted magician just as easily as I could be an obscure one? I pictured myself touring Europe, including a command performance for Queen Victoria.

15

Daydreams, of course, but they could become a reality; some day dreams do. Magic wasn't overdone like some branches of show business. According to magic dealers' catalogs anyone could be a magician. Few were doing it. The main requirement was a magic catalog from which to select and order the needed apparatus. The dealers supplied instructions with tricks and guaranteed that anyone could perform them. A little money and plenty of nerve were also needed. I had both, especially the "little money." I knew all this, but what I didn't know was that the dime museum performer wasn't paid $100 a week. I was very misinformed about this. I learned later that in many cases such performers did not receive enough for room, board, and transportation to the next stand. Furthermore, I didn't know that while Herrmann's receipts were thousands of dollars a week, in some instances they were not sufficient to cover the cost of transportation on three private railway cars, theater rent, extensive advertising, and the salaries of the many assistants required to assist in giving the show. This was a real situation where ignorance was bliss. The question of money did not bother me because I had a small bank account. It was not enough to finance a magic show, but I did not know this either. It seems that I did not know much of anything, although I thought I did.

I induced a relative, C. K. Reichert by name, to invest enough money to purchase apparatus from Martinka and Company of New York. As most of the items had to be made to order, it took several months before I received them. While waiting I had some stationery printed, proclaiming me to be "The Premier American Conjurer and Illusionist." Just what prompted me to consider that title appropriate for me is a mystery I never have been able to solve, because I could not even give a show. I had no lady assistant, so I used a picture of a girl acquaintance and had a halftone made, which I used to embellish my letterhead. As her father was a clergyman, she did not want her name used. I billed her as Miss Lulu Armstrong. Still having some time to wait for the apparatus to arrive I decided to arrange for some theatre bookings, and from a theatrical publication I obtained the names and addresses of a number of theatres throughout the Midwest. By the aid of a well worded letter and contract I managed to book 75 one to three night shows. I booked these dates for the next theatrical season, about nine months in advance of the show date.

Finally, the apparatus arrived. One good look at the complicated magical paraphernalia convinced me that I did not know as much about magic as I thought I did. I tried to understand the instructions, but they were so confusing and full of technicalities that I could not comprehend what they meant. I discovered I was not a magician. A ton of apparatus, some nice stationery and a stylish full dress suit did not qualify me as one, any more than some brushes and paint make an artist or some musical instruments make a musician. I was now concerned with those 75 contracts I had signed, agreeing to be on hand at a specified date to give a show. In alarm I wrote to the theatres cancelling the engagements, giving as a reason that Miss Armstrong was ill. I received an avalanche of protesting letters from infuriated house managers. One complained that he had missed booking a large city show because I had a date contracted for during the week they wanted. Another demanded proof that Miss Armstrong was ill. Still another threatened suit. I could not prove Miss Armstrong's illness because there was no such person and she could not have been sick. I could see myself going to jail for life. I ignored the letters and heard no more about the matter. I had to discontinue my plans for a big show in the near future as I was not able to give one and my finances were at a low ebb. I did not have sufficient funds to conduct any kind of a show, large or small.

Though I temporarily had to give up the idea of a big show, I did not cease in my efforts at being a magician. I studied the apparatus carefully, purchased a dictionary to assist in translating the egregious words used in the instructions, and finally, after a lot of practice, was able to exhibit a few tricks. I showed wherever I could and whenever I could get a chance to do so. The few friends who witnessed my pitiful attempts praised me highly, saying I was equal to the great Herrmann, that some day I would startle the world, etc. Like any other amateur, I believed every word they said. At one place I worked without a stage. This seemed to me to be a cheap and unprofessional way of giving a show. I was careful not to allow any friends see me doing it, as I felt most humiliated. Years later, night spots inaugurated floor shows and they are now considered quite proper. At other times I gave shows in saloons. Milwaukee was full of saloons which had dance halls which could be used for entertainment. These were the places I worked in for the most part. This was another degrading situation. In the present day, high–class saloons under another name employ expert magicians to entertain their customers. The modern booze joint is decorated with color and chrome, but a camouflaged saloon by any other name smells just as bad, even if the tricks performed are excellent.

Then I encountered a fortunate circumstance. Mr. Berthold Herr, a manufacturer of wax figures who also had a small stage show in his museum, booked a magician for the week by the name of Professor Vandez. I immediately made the acquaintance of the Professor. He was a very pleasant gentleman and offered to give me all the help he could. Those pieces of my apparatus which I could not understand he explained to me, and he even allowed me to take his place and give a few shows – bad ones. I finally managed to acquire enough skill to be able to present a fifteen minute show. With this act I played engagements in and around Milwaukee for five years.

I was delegated to the cellar of the wax works, where tallow candles with pie tins for reflectors served as footlights. The atmosphere was only a degree removed from a children's barn or woodshed show, but the surroundings were probably not any worse than the shows I gave. Articles I had concealed popped into view, some of which I dropped because I was nervous or clumsy. A hidden rooster made his place of concealment known by squawking. I loaded a glass of water in a breast pocket, an egg under my vest on one side and a silk handkerchief on the other side. The center table had a drape reaching to the floor. During the performance, the egg fell on the floor and rolled under the table drape. The glass of water followed suit, and I kicked it under the table. The red silk handkerchief peeped out from under my vest and I had to omit that trick. I had a funnel pistol but no blank cartridges, although the resourceful Professor Vandez told me how to overcome that difficulty. He advised me to snap the trigger, and when the pistol didn't fire,to say, "Well, the pistol didn't go, but the trick goes just the same." I followed his advice. As no hissing occurred and no one threw ancient eggs at me, in my ignorance I thought I gave a good show. When the professor terminated his engagement, I took charge of the museum.

On exhibition were several excellent life sized wax figures. One was of the first man to be executed by electricity, strapped to an especially made heavy wooden chair. With a heavy black blindfold, it was a gruesome looking object. Another exhibit was a dying soldier. This was a figure of a wounded soldier lying on his back, with a bloody bandage around his head. His breast, actuated by clockwork, moved as though he were breathing. Beside him knelt a praying man with bowed head. The prize piece was a Sleeping Beauty, a reclining figure of a pretty, well dressed girl which also had a breath mechanism in its chest. The only wax work about these dummies was the head and hands. The parts covered by clothing were made of wooden frame work, covered with heavy paper or sometimes papier mache. I lectured about the creations, explaining what they were to the patrons. In order to make the Sleeping Beauty more impressive I always said, "This is one of the most expensive wax figures ever made. Expensive because it is made of wax throughout. It is the custom to slight the parts covered with clothing; however, this figure is made entirely of wax." This story (lie) always made a good impression on my listeners, that is until the day a somewhat inebriated young woman reached over the enclosing railing, lifted the long skirt, and exposed the crude legs and body. This furnished amusement for the patrons. It did not worry me much, and I repeated the statement at the next lecture an hour later. I was still employed at the dry goods store, and as I did not want anyone to find out what I was doing at the museum, I worked under the name of Professor Sharp. I worked at the museum Saturdays, Sundays, and some evenings.

By this time I had learned to use all of the apparatus and considered myself capable of giving a full evening's show. I booked a little town about fifteen minutes from Milwaukee. To be exact, it was Menomonee Falls. I had a girl assistant but needed a man to sell tickets and to attend to the all important money end of the show. He went to the town by train, but as my show was not packed for train transportation, the girl and I went there via horse and a small wagon. It was an ordinary type of mid-winter day. I set up the show, and at about five in the afternoon I went to the City Clerk to pay the license fee which was one dollar. At this time the temperature was dropping and it was spitting snow. By the time we had finished our evening meal there was a full time blizzard on. We made our way to the hall with difficulty, and as the storm increased in fury it became almost impossible for people to attend the show. I gave a performance for a very few people, not taking in enough to pay expenses, so I was out my hall rent, license fee, hotel and livery bill. Wondering what kind of an impression I had made, I listened for comments after the show. I heard one man say, "Bill, how'd you like the show tonight?" Said Bill, "Hell, I wish I'd saved my money and spent it for beer." Not very encouraging. I consoled myself with the thought that Barnum and Bailey's Greatest Show on Earth was frequently harshly criticized. Next morning the snow was very deep. The girl and I drove back to Milwaukee in the open wagon. Fortunately, the hotel lady had been solicitous enough to provide us with a jug of hot water to keep our feet warm. As soon as I reached the Milwaukee city limit I put the girl on a mule pulled streetcar so she might arrive home before she expired. This was not a very encouraging beginning for an ambitious magician.

I was still conceited enough to think myself able to give a show as good as Herrmann's, so when that gentleman came to Milwaukee again I decided to apply to him for a position in his show. I had no difficulty in obtaining an interview with him at his hotel, the Plankinton House. He was most gracious and affable but could not give me a position in the show as he kept the same people from year to year and seldom made any changes. He could, however, give me a job running a calcium light in the balcony of the theatre. This light was used in Madam Herrmann's spectacular dance. I didn't want to be a light operator, I wanted to be a magician. So the interview was over. At another time I had a similar experience with Harry Kellar in Chicago. I had made the acquaintance of two of the world's most noted magicians, and that was quite an accomplishment for an amateur magician.

With the experience I acquired I became more proficient in my work and gave entertainment for churches, schools, clubs, and social gatherings. For a while I worked without pay. I was my city's first and worst professional magician. Still determined to be a noted magician, I quit my job at the dry goods store to go on the road. The owner of the store said he admired the nerve I showed in quitting a good job. He said that as long as I worked for him I was sure of coffee and doughnuts every morning, while if I went out into the unfriendly world there was no telling what I might have, if anything. With my good appetite this friendly advice did not encourage me, but it did not frighten me, either. I packed my effects in trunks and started out. My friends predicted I would come back dead broke in a few weeks. They were mistaken. I did not come back for two years, and I was not broke. I had twelve dollars, just enough to pay railroad fare to a town for another start.

I travelled for a few years with medicine shows. There was the Kickapoo Indian Medicine Company, the Unatilla Indian Medicine Company, the Warm Springs Medicine Company, the Shaker Medicine Company, the Quaker Medicine Company, and others. While these small amusements were not the aristocrats of the showbusiness, they did enable me to obtain plenty of the experience I needed. For a while I operated one of them myself in company with a man named Harry B. Clark. We ran for a year to successful business; I made $250 in 1899. However, as conditions around the show were not very harmonious I decided to quit and conduct my own show. I needed a girl to work in illusions, so to make sure I would be able to keep her I married one on September 6, 1901.

As soon as I had my wife sufficiently rehearsed I went on the road with a three-day show. I would stay in a town a week, spending the first three days in advertising and the last three days in giving the show. The feature items were the Aerial Suspension, the Substitution Trunk Mystery and the Spirit Cabinet Act. I had seen the suspension act on the Midway of the 1892 Chicago World's Fair, and when I did the act I would say, "You may have seen me perform this at the 1892 World's Fair." Many people came up to me afterwards and told me they had seen me do it there. I also had a fine assortment of small tricks, and my wife sang illustrated songs which were popular at the time. Business was not good. I showed fair sized towns and reasonably good theatres. Receipts were generally just about enough to cover expenses; sometimes not enough. This wasn't satisfactory, and when my wife became ill I sent her home to her mother and I joined a medicine show in western New York.

The owner of the show was L. H. Cooper. He was a good musician and carried some first-class vaudeville performers; his show was one of unusual merit. For advertising purposes he had a monkey, which he would place in front of the theatre to attract attention. It was the winter season, and to keep the monkey warm during the night he kept a lighted lantern in the cage. One night the theatre caught fire and burned to the ground. As there was no other fire in the building at three o'clock in the morning, the supposition was that the monkey upset the lantern.

I had been studying Spanish and was thinking of going to Mexico or South America, but now I had lost everything I owned. My best clothes and my money were destroyed. I had nothing but the contents of a hotel satchel and was wearing my oldest suit of work clothes. I thought the end of the world had come, but it hadn't. Friends rallied to my support; some loaned me money. August Roterberg, the Chicago dealer in magical apparatus, let me have some goods on credit. A printer furnished me with advertising. My old partner had purchased a magical outfit which he was unable to use and he asked me to come and work for him and use his apparatus. This I did, and I gradually replaced my own equipment. I never realized I had so many friends. In two weeks I was on the road again.

As my new equipment was not as good as that which had burned, I did not care to play good theatres. I decided to play some small villages and to stay a week instead of three days. I opened in a little place of about one hundred in population. It could hardly be called a town or even a village. It consisted of a store, a one-room school, a church, and three dwellings. The place did not even have a name. The hall was without scenery and had only a small stage. I had to hang cloth curtains. The lighting was poor. I stayed a week in that place and had a good crowd every night. I made more clear profit there than I had ever made in the larger places with the good outfit. I was told by experienced showmen who played these small places that they had not been over showed, that expense in them would be very low, and that there was always a profit to be made even though it might not be a large one. This suited me exactly. I wanted to *always* make a profit. I had been working for several years and almost *never* made a profit. The thought of being able to put money in my money belt interested me above all else. I had decided to play some very small places until I could bring my outfit back to its original standard, and while I did not like the idea of showing in the sticks, I did like the money saving idea. So I tackled the brush heaps, as the small places were called, and I played no other kind for more than fifty years.

My wife returned and brought with her a baby boy. That's why she went home. She and I practiced on some talking comedy acts to add to the show. When all was in readiness we started out again with a two-person show. Transportation in those days between small towns was mostly horse and wagon for the trunks, and horse and buggy for the people. There were only dirt highways, and in wet weather the dirt was mud and movement was slow. During the winter season going across country in an open buggy was a hardship and not healthy for a woman and small baby.

The baby, named Francis, was never a healthy child and died during the winter season in a small town near Toledo, Ohio. I closed the show and took him to a town in northern Michigan for burial. Then we went back to Ohio and continued showing in small places for several years. About this time I had an explosion of acetylene gas which severely burned my face and left hand; fortunately I was able to secure immediate medical attendance and the burns healed without leaving a scar. My wife didn't like the rugged road life and wanted to go home to live with her mother. In 1908 we were divorced. From then until 1920 I managed to keep the small show going with the aid of hired assistants. Then I married again. My first wife was a good looking, sweet, demure, bashful country girl. She was the Maude Miller type who raked the meadow sweet with hay. When I first saw her she was sitting on the porch of a modest little home, reading a Bible in preparation for her Sunday School class. She sang in the choir and was active in church affairs. Truly an 18-carat find, but an unsuccessful marriage. My second wife was working with a carnival concession when I met her. This was not an ideal place to find a good wife, but I took another chance and won. She proved to be one of the finest women that God ever placed on this earth. Her birth place was Allegan, Michigan. Her name was Mabel. I added a motion picture show to my program, and Mabel was able to do some specialties of her own. She was talented, and with her I was able to give some really first class entertainment.

By this time I had put in about twenty-five years in the show business. Travelling and showing conditions had changed during these years. The horse and buggy days were over, and I owned an automobile. My first car had been an Oldsmobile which I got in trade for a movie projector in 1910, but the first car that proved to be of any practical value was the Model T Ford I bought in 1920. Travelling by auto was easier than the horse and buggy, and paved highways were making their appearance. In cold or rainy weather the closed car was warm. I used a tent to show in during warm weather, and this was better than showing in dirty, empty store buildings. Also, I now had better lighting. A friend of mine, William Hannaman living at Winneconne, Wisconsin, was an expert mechanic and electrician. He had a show similar to mine but with better music and moving pictures. For no good reason at all he built me an electric light plant powered by the engine of my Ford. He also built a house car and two trailers which could be converted into a stage for the tent. With the addition of this extra equipment, especially the lighting system, my outfit was better than ever and the overall appearance of my tent was improved.

For the next twenty years Mabel and I travelled over big stretches of territory, mostly in the Central states, although we did also visit the East, West and South. We showed in Illinois, Indiana, Iowa, Kansas, Michigan, Minnesota, Missouri, Nebraska, New York, Ohio, Pennsylvania and Wisconsin, with jumps into Arkansas and Kentucky. About the best section for business was the state of Wisconsin. On the whole, the residents there seemed to be more industrious and prosperous than in other states. I am speaking of the farmers upon whose patronage I principally depended. I showed the territory around Shawano, Wisconsin every summer for sixteen years. As the state had cool temperatures in the summer it was fine for the tent business. The winters were cold and I was forced to go South during those seasons. Usually I went to Tennessee. I liked that state and liked the fine people who lived there. The temperatures were mild and the spring season came along early. Mabel loved the show life, especially the outdoor tent season. Along about 1938 she commenced to show signs of a lowering vitality. Despite a weakened constitution, she insisted on carrying on her part in the show. She was not sick for any great length of time when she died on February 5, 1941 in Kalamazoo, Michigan. A good soul had gone to rest.

This left me alone again. I went back to Tennessee, and for about two years I showed alone. When World War II came along, I was unable to obtain enough gasoline to run my autos or to obtain tires for replacement. There was nothing I could do but close my show. I stored the outfit.

I went to Nashville, Tennessee, seeking employment. I found it at the first place I applied. I became manager of the Star Hotel, and I remained there five years. It was a most pleasant occupation. Mr. C. R. Dowland owned a chain of small hotels and the Star was one of them. Miss Grace Dumwright was general manager of the hotels. Mr. Dowland and Miss Grace, as we called her, were friendly employers, and my engagement there was most satisfactory. It has been ten years since I left and I still correspond with them; at Christmas time I received a lovely present. Miss Grace is now Mrs. C. R. Dowland. When the hotel passed into other hands I lost my job and moved to Michigan.

Colon, Michigan is only thirty-five miles from Kalamazoo. Colon is noted for several things. One is that it is the home of Blackstone, the great magician. Another is that it has the largest factory in the world making magical apparatus, the Abbott Magical Manufacturing Company. And finally, Colon is noted for being composed of a fine lot of citizens.

I went out one day to visit the Abbott Magical Company and they gave me a job. Abbott's was a wonderful place to work. The work was easy and pleasant; and Mr. Abbott and his partner, Recil Bordner, were two agreeable men to work for. I felt as though I belonged to their family. I had a standing invitation to come to their homes at anytime for a meal. Mrs. Abbott and Mrs. Bordner were the same kind of people. We called Mrs. Abbott, Gladys, and Mrs. Bordner was Donna. We also called Mr. Abbott, Percy, and Mr. Bordner, Recil. If I ever met as fine a quartet I don't remember where.

The Abbott plant consisted of seven separate buildings: the plastic shop, the paint shop, the metal shop, print shop, wood shop, one large show room, office and warehouse. I worked in Number 7. This was the place where many of the small tricks were made. I worked on over 60 of them. They made over 1,000 items. Mr. Good presided over this shop. He was just what his name implied; we called him "Goodie." All employees had been with the Abbott Company for years. Fred and Carolyn Merrill, who were once with the Blackstone show, were old employees. Howard Melson (Mel) came for an engagement of 6 weeks and remained for 18 years. Irene Elliot, the first person to be employed by Mr. Abbott, had been there for over 25 years. During the 5 years that I was there, not one employee left or was discharged. Truly a fine place to work.

Each year the Abbott Company held a convention or get together. The first one was held in some kind of a shed or crude building with an attendance of 18. Each year the number attending increased, until in recent years there were over 1,000 and the largest auditorium obtainable was not able to hold them. For many years they were held in a large tent seating over 1,000. When the metal shop burned, the tent went with it. Magicians and laity came from all over the world to attend these conventions. A big delegation from London was often in attendance.

Percy booked expensive acts for his shows, bringing them from all quarters of the globe. A lot of the activities were held out-of-doors with beautiful lakes in view. This open air affair was a pleasing departure from the stuffy indoor meetings of the cities, although in case of rain there was always plenty of tent and building shelter. At one of the conventions I gave a show. I thought an old time magic show would be a novelty. I had been giving shows for over fifty years, and all of my tricks were of ancient vintage. I broached the matter to Percy, and he said to go ahead and use the big tent some afternoon.

I resurrected a pair of knee breeches, long silk stockings, buckled slippers, dickey, winged collar, large black bow tie, and a short tailed dress coat. If I had put on a goatee, mustache, and black wig I would have been the picture of Herrmann. I used my tables with the old style drapes. I showed only the old-time tricks of Herrmann and Kellar. For large effects, I showed the Bewitched Organ Pipes and the Anna Eva Fay Spirit Cabinet. The audience was composed of magicians only, about 600 of them. I was frightened at having to perform for such a critical audience, but it proved to be one of my finest. The trick which puzzled them the most was the growth of flowers in the cornucopia. Everyone knew the mechanics of the trick, but not everyone knew the method I used for introducing the folded flowers into the cone. I learned it by watching Kellar. I made and filled the cone six times. No one seemed to detect the method I used for loading, and they became so excited that they rose and applauded. I think it was the most applause that I ever received. The peculiar part of it was that the principle I employed in loading the cone was one that is known to every magician. They simply did not know or realize that I was using it.

Although I made no charge for giving the show, I was well paid for it. After it was over, John Mulholland and Ed Dart took up money collections which were given to me. I stood in the Abbott show room and people would shake hands and congratulate me, at the same time leaving a dollar bill in my hand. Some would push a bill down the back of my neck. Others would place money in my pockets or shove some into my pants at the waist. I had to go home and undress to find it all. The total amount was well over one hundred dollars. I could never comprehend what was so good about that show. I can only reason that all the conditions must have been right. The temperature and humidity must have been comfortable, and the stars and planets must have been in benevolent positions. Everyone was sober, and with such an array of agreeable circumstances, anyone could give a good show.

When I left Colon I went to Kalamazoo and held the position of desk clerk at the Library Park Hotel for a year. Failing eye sight necessitated an operation to remove cataracts. This proved to be successful, and I now have good vision again. I was now in my eighties (nearly ninety) and was finishing my seventieth year in magic. I wondered if I hadn't better retire. I not only wondered about it, I did.

I had spent my boyhood days in Milwaukee and had many friends there. For five years I had been employed by Landauer and Company, a wholesale dry goods and notion house; and during this time I had become acquainted with most of the city's merchants. During the same five years I had also worked nights at Vizay's Dancing academy, where I had met about 5,000 girl and boy patrons. When not engaged with these occupations, I had given local magic shows, and from these about 5,000 older people knew me by sight. Also, there were a number of relatives. I thought I would be well acquainted in that city. Well, I moved there, and having been gone for over 50 years I am unable to locate a single person who knew or remembered me. They are all dead, or if alive are in wheelchairs or hospitals or on their way to the undertaker. That's one of the disadvantages of living to a ripe old age; one has to hear of the deaths of his friends, go to their funerals, and buy flowers. I feel like a man without a country again, the same as I was when I was a little boy. But I have always been able to make friends and will continue to do so.

Most of my friends are younger than I am. I like to be associated with younger people. That's why I don't go to the old folk's home. I enjoy the company of two or three people of my own age, but I do not care to be mixed up with 50 or 100 of them. About all they can do is to sit around, look miserable, and gripe about their aches and pains; or else, try to justify themselves for not being wealthy, generally putting the blame onto the woman they married. For a change, each one wonders who will be the next to die. That's why I am living in a furnished room and going to a restaurant for my meals.

I am used to such a life because for eighty-five years I

never had a permanent home, and I have much to keep me busy. I live near the public library and have about a million books at my command. I am also near to the Museum of Natural History, and as I am interested in such matters, I go there. I have many friends in all parts of the world and have an extensive correspondence. I go to night school and study Spanish. I spend some time in church to atone for my sins, real or imaginary. When there is nothing else to do, I sit in the cool park and solve crossword puzzles. Not so bad at that, is it?

I am in good physical condition, and my physician tells me that I might live another ten years. Wow! If the world advances as rapidly in the next decade as it has in the past, I dislike contemplating where we will be. I would like to live just long enough, though, to enjoy cheap transportation to the moon, so that I could go there and find out at firsthand if it is really made of green cheese, or if that was a fairy story I believed when I was a child.

CHAPTER TWO

HORSE AND BUGGY DAYS

My life as a showman began in the good old horse and buggy days of the 1880s and 1890s. I do not know what these days were good for; they did, however, give the livery man a chance to earn an honest living by renting decrepit old horses and broken down buggies to those unfortunates needing transportation. The decade of the 80s was very quiet and should be termed "the Tame 80s"— they were so calm and peaceful that most persons were in bed and asleep by nine in the evening. To remain away from home later than that was almost a crime. Streets were poorly lighted, and one could hardly move around unless the moon was full. Those who could afford it carried a lantern. Conditions were ideal for lawbreakers to operate, and they did. The next ten years are termed "the Gay '90s." All that I can remember about them that was gay is gramophones, barber shop quartets, kissing parties, and sleigh bells. Occasionally we had a taffy pull. Also good during those days were beer, whiskey and chewing gum — I am writing this from hearsay, as I had no experience with those commodities. I very much remember these: bad highways; cold hotels; bathtubless houses; firetrap heaters; unsanitary stores; outdoor toilets; painful dentistry; odious barrooms; germ catching whiskers; deceptive advertising; plug tobacco and cuspidors; town drunks; tramps; militant teachers; child labor; consumption; rheumatism; gout; fake doctors; asafetida bags; wood and coal fires; coal oil lamps; dirty restaurants; cold, mule-drawn streetcars; loose boards in sidewalks; underfed, overworked and abused horses; 12-

31

hour workdays; diseased meat; contaminated water; etc. There might have been diaper rash, though I never heard of it. This is an abbreviated overall picture of what was not so gay during "the Gay '90s."

The good old days had a few advantages, though, in spite of all this. We had what we called a free country. We had a free press; and even though a radical editor or two might be shot by irresponsible persons, there were always other radical editors waiting to take their places, and the press continued to be free. We could rob birds' nests and kill birds to be used as ornaments on women's hats. We could read dime novels and sometimes could even be buried alive. We could carry dangerous fire-arms, and shoot firecrackers on the Fourth and blow off a couple of fingers. If we did, it was nobody's business but our own. We could buy plenty of morphine for a dime. We could work twelve hours a day for as little pay as we pleased, and there was no one around to force us to work less or ask more. We could spend our money, if we had any, taking a chance with lotteries. Nobody ever won, but we were kept out of mischief by being busy thinking of the mischief we could get into if we did win. Better than anything, we could wear derby hats without being laughed at.

Cigarettes were smoked in the past, and boys and men had yellow finger tips the same as they do now. Long-faced reformers launched tirades against the habit, but it seemed that the more they bellowed, the more the smokers smoked. Little boys in the country made cigarettes out of newspaper and corn silk. City boys made theirs out of newspaper, dried grass, or anything that would burn. These ancient youngsters were the originators of the roll your own system. If girls or women smoked at that time, they did it behind the woodshed or in the backhouse. A package of pimp sticks, as they were sometimes termed, contained a small photo of an actress in tights. This, of course, was a very immoral procedure and was vigorously denounced by the self-appointed moralists. The photos continued to circulate. One great argument against cigarette smoking was that it caused disease and early deaths;

in other words, it killed people. It was said that every cigarette smoked was another nail in the smoker's coffin. Coffin nails, they called them. It was true that many people smoked daily, and equally true that many people died every day. It is also true that people who never smoked a cigarette, or even saw one, are dying daily, and that they are just as dead as the ones who did smoke.

In the 1920s, many women acquired the smoking habit. There are arguments for and against the practice. In the hill country I heard a woman voice her opinion on the subject. Her daughter, Lucy, said, "Maw, is they enything wrong with girls smokin' cigarettes?" "No, they ain't nothin' really wrong," said Maw, "only what you do to your mouth when you smoke cigarettes. You got a mouthful of terbaccer ends, paper, slimy snot, soot from smoke, and rotten vittels, jest about what is in a spittoon, and you might jest as well take a drink outen one 'cause your mouth smells and tastes like one and no nice young feller wants to kiss a mouth like that. No, there ain't nothin' wrong any more than there is in pickin' your nose or scratching your backside, but you wouldn't want folks to ketch you doin' it, now would you?" I might add that while Maw would not smoke a cigarette, she did "dip" snuff.

I never engaged in the practices of drinking, smoking, gambling, or other activities requiring the expenditure of money. I did drink a little beer at one time, but I was cured of that habit. I had my eye on a nice girl, but she did not pay much attention to me. She told a friend why, and the friend told me. She said that I drank beer, and when I came near her, I had an odor about me like a swill barrel. I quit drinking beer, but that did not do me any good, because I did not get the girl. I never learned to drink other intoxicants because a physician told me that liquor used as a beverage was harmful to the average person but if used in small quantities as a stimulant was beneficial, especially for elderly persons whose strength was commencing to wane. As I wanted to be in good physical condition when I became classified as an elderly person and didn't want to be afflicted with waning strength at any time,

I abstained from drinking intoxicants all my life. Now that I have arrived at that period of life when I am an elderly person of waning strength and could use a little whiskey to good advantage, I find that its price makes my use of it prohibitive. I never learned to chew tobacco because I tried it once when I was nine years of age. In about ten minutes, I acquired a violent dislike for chewing tobacco. I read in a magazine that the average man spent in a lifetime enough money for cigars and smoking tobacco to pay for a house. So, in order to be able to own a house when I became old, I did not smoke during my lifetime. I have now arrived at an age which some consider old. Do I own a house? I do not.

I never learned to use profanity because when I was a little boy in an orphan asylum I used a bad word, probably "damn." The sister who heard it gave me a harsh scolding and said that to purify my mouth she would have to wash out the bad word. She used a dirty rag and strong yellow laundry soap. She must have done a perfect job, as I have not uttered a bad word since. At the present time, profanity appears to be necessary for some people's very existence. If one does not swear, he is considered a nobody. Someone has said, "Look out for people who don't smoke, drink or swear; for although they do not have these particular faults, they are liable to have others that are much worse." Maybe so; I just would not know.

There were no alcoholics in those pre-historical days. When a person became intoxicated, he was termed a drunk. Every saloon keeper took care of his own drunks by putting them on a cot in a backroom allowing them to sleep it off. As soon as they regained consciousness most of them automatically started to acquire another jag. Today they are called alcoholics; this does not, however, seem to reduce the number of drunks.

The saloons of the '80s and '90s were respectable places when compared with present taverns and nightspots. The saloons of that period were patronized by men only. Objectionable women had other haunts of their own and kept their unsavory reputation in their own environments. Some sa-

34

loons had a family entrance. This was a side door entrance to a room apart from the saloon proper. Here a man could take his wife and children. Children were never given intoxicants. They had to be satisfied with soda water. The conversation in the saloons was sometimes rough, but if a woman or child happened to enter the place all vulgar talk and profanity instantly ceased.

Juvenile delinquency had not been invented at the time of which I am writing, and so there was no problem. Undoubtedly there were juveniles and some of them must have been delinquent, but little attention was paid to them. Older people were busy attending to their own affairs, like playing checkers, dominos, chewing tobacco, and other superannuated activities. The juveniles committed their delinquencies behind the barn or in some other sequestered spot which rendered their conduct invisible. Those angels of the "Gay '90s" were clever, if ignorant and unsophisticated.

Some women who were not juveniles were slightly in error in some of their activities. Their favorite sport was trying to inveigle Civil War veterans into marriage. No matter if the old fellows were three times their age and had two heads and a leg missing, if they received as much as 35 dollars a month pension, they were considered wealthy and a desirable "catch" by the girls. Many veterans were caught and most of them did not live long. Another thing we did not have in the "bad" old days was a beauty shop. Every girl was her own beautician. Material for make up was not plentiful, so some girls had to use makeshift methods. For powder they used cornstarch, and for rouge they dampened some red tissue paper, which they dabbed on their cheeks. This would give them a pinkish tinge somewhat akin to an anemic sunset. To blacken their eyebrows they used the charred ends of half burnt matches. For no good reason at all, they put a beauty spot on one cheek. Total cost of material was about two cents. If all this did not conceal the pimples, then add a veil.

Farmers were a most contented class of people, despite the disadvantages of farming at that time. They worked from sunrise to sunset. They were the earliest exploiters of day-light savings time. They cradled their grain and cut grass with a scythe, using muscle power. They sold eggs for ten cents a dozen and butter at the same price per pound. They travelled by horse and lumber wagon once a week to the nearest town to purchase groceries and get their mail includ-ing the weekly newspaper. Many used homemade tallow candles for illumination. They drew their water from a well with a bucket and a rope. Medical service was far away. Educational opportunities were limited.

The family horse was just what the name implies, one of the family and, in most cases, it was treated as such. Old Dobbin seemed to be human and to have a soul. He was loved by the children and pampered by the oldsters. The young lover depended on him when he wanted to take his girl for a buggy ride. Once out on a country road, he could tie lines around the whip and use both arms and hands for any purpose that suited him. A story was told of one young couple who fell asleep in each other's arms. The horse plodded slowly along and brought them into the village at sunrise. Early risers found them asleep in the buggy, with the horse at the public watering trough vainly trying to release the check rein so it could reach the water. No high-priced, modern automobile, no matter what its length, how much chrome it has or how handsome the salesman can furnish such super service.

There were no refrigerators then. We had ice boxes, ice men and plenty of jokes about the ice man and the house wife. These jokes became so numerous that some husbands re-mained at home until the ice man had left. This did not change the situation, because there was always the possibility of the ice man returning. There were no washing machines, the washing being done by a washerwoman operating with a tub and board. There were no jokes about these ladies, and the man of the house could go to work on washday.

There were cameras and real amateur photographers. We sensitized and developed our own plates before films were known. We sunprinted, toned, mounted, and burnished our positives. Today an amateur photographer presses a button, then sends the film to a professional photographer who does the actual work. The amateur exhibits the prints as his own creation when all he did was to press a lousy little button.

We were the original "Do it Yourselfers." Everyone had to be able to do his own work. One could not telephone for a carpenter to come and tighten a screw because there were telephones only in the large city business houses. A person had to tighten his own screws, and be his own carpenter, painter, blacksmith, mason, and glazier, etc., as most people did not have money enough to pay others to do their odd jobs for them.

We were not aware that psychologists had not been invented at that time. Nobody knew what psychology meant. For that matter, very few people of today know what it means. It is a word like "politics" or "propaganda." Everybody uses them, but few can define them.

There were many so-called patent medicines which cured every disease which did or did not exist. With half of the population awakening every morning with no appetite, halitosis, B.O., headaches, colds, and stomach ulcers, there will always be a sale among credulous people for these concoctions. The remedies used as home remedies were simple ones, such as turpentine, baking soda, and castor oil. Sometimes they were as effective as the modern, expensive wonder drugs. One thing is certain; when a user of a wonder drug dies, he is just as dead as if he had used the simpler kind.

There were no babysitters then, because it was easier to give the baby a dose of laudanum. This would put the kid (we did not call them kids then) to sleep for four hours or until it developed another belly ache, when it would be given another dose of the narcotic drug. This was cheaper and more reliable than paying a girl. I hope the present day sitters do not take advantage of this information and take a bottle of laudanum with them on the job. They probably will not, however, as laudanum is not easily obtained at the present time.

We had shows that were shows, and none were mechanical. Motion pictures had not been invented. We had vaudeville, dramas, concerts, minstrels, and burlesque shows. The latter were termed "leg shows," although the legs did not show. The legs were there, all right, but were covered by silk or cotton tights. The legs were owned by voluptuous women of generous avoirdupois. Reformers considered these exhibitions to be the height of indecency. They would make periodic complaints to the police, who would periodically order the legs to be covered with proper clothing. The show people would then clothe the girls' legs, the table legs, the piano legs, the chair legs, and even the dog's legs. In a short time, the police order would be forgotten, the tights would reappear, and the cycle would start all over again. Today one can walk down the street and see all the naked legs one cares about, and one does not have to pay for the privilege. The legs might not be of the high standard of those shown by the leg show women, but they are legs, nevertheless. The minstrel shows consisted principally of a brass band street parade and about thirty burnt cork blackened performers who sang and told jokes. The jokes must have been good, as they are still being used by entertainers. All of these forms of entertainment would be much appreciated by present day audiences if we could find capable artists to give them.

Those shows and performers faded away with the coming of the machine made shows, the movie, the talkie, and the television. The present day public does not know that anything better than this ever existed. About the only advantage the piped into the home show has is the fact that the listeners and viewers can make unkind remarks about the quality of the performance, and the actors can't hear them. Thus, there is no chance for the actors to be pelted with stale eggs and old tomatoes. This should sometimes be done, especially when they conclude an 1855 drama with a long, drawn out, sloppy weather, cow pulling its foot out of the mudhole kiss. That style of kiss had not been invented in the year 1855.

In spite of all the disadvantages, people of that time thought they were enjoying a high standard of living. They had so many things that the people before them did not have that they could not imagine anything better. When the electric light, telephone and phonograph came along their happiness knew no bounds. There were vague rumors of horseless carriages, flying machines and underwater boats. These ideas were dismissed as the products of a disorganized imagination. Time has proven that they were.

The small town showman circa 1892

CHAPTER THREE

SMALL TOWNS

I played small towns, up to a population of five thousand, staying a week in each place. They had fairly good country theatres where I played for a percentage of the receipts, which were never very large. Many people in small towns were antagonistic to shows — some because of radical religious principles, some because of poverty, some because of prejudices, and some because they did not believe in shows.

I do not know just who originated the idea of having our fair land disfigured by so many small towns when cities, with so many greater disadvantages, would have been more satisfactory. I showed in towns for nearly sixty years and never went farther than ten miles to find another one. I never liked small towns. I should not complain about them, though, because for over half-a-century they were the means of my livelihood. They may have been short on convenience, but there was always an abundance of fresh air, sunshine and enough to eat, most of the time. Also some money.

Small towns of the old days were easily detected. I would drive along the country road until I came to a collection of old buildings. If an inspection revealed them to be farm buildings I would drive on. If I saw something that looked like a dirty little store with a dirty man sitting in a chair chewing tobacco in front of it, I could be reasonably sure that I had found a small town or village. If I could see a few hitching posts and a one-room school house, I could be sure I had found one. Sometimes they were a little larger, with an extra business building and a church. Then I knew I had discovered a real rural metropolis.

41

"Town" is not really the proper name for most of the places I showed in. Some of them were not even villages or hamlets. They were just wide places on the road, and consisted of a store with several houses near it. These places had no post office and were not shown on any map. Any names they may have had were colloquial and of uncertain origin. Many names were peculiar, like Crack Pot, Buckskin, Barbed Wire, Gun Barrel, Onion Patch, Frog Jump, Cross Roads, Back Ache, and Dirty Creek. Sometimes I located in places a little larger with nice sounding names like Silverwood, Rose Lawn, Goldendale, Sweet Pea, Sun Set, and Silver Valley. The smaller places with the hick names were always the best for business, while those slightly larger towns with the pretty names would be a fizzle.

If there was one thing more than another which was prominent among all small town natives, it was their bump of curiosity; and if there was one thing that I could do better than anything else, it was to be secretive and keep my private affairs concealed from the public. Regarding my personal affairs, they were mostly interested in knowing my age and how much money I took in. They never found out. When a chin whiskered individual would ask me point blank, "How old ye be?" I would answer, "I don't know." Then I would explain that my parents died when I was very young and that I had lived among strangers who never told me my age. I would add that I was not quite sure if I knew my correct name. In answer to the amount of money I took in, I would say that I never counted it and that I never kept accounts. I was obliged to keep the secrets of my tricks and illusions from becoming public knowledge, because when the secret of a trick was known, its entertainment value dropped to a low, low, low. Some people would follow me to the next town to see a trick performed again, hoping to detect the mechanics. Some tricks had several methods by which they could be performed; and when I saw too many persons from the previous town in the audience, I changed my method of working and was able to deceive them again. As I had such a large repertoire of tricks,

I could also give them a new show. Sometimes they would wrongly imagine that they had detected the secret of a trick. This always suited me better than if they had imagined right. The popular idea of strings, traps and mirrors was as widespread at that time as it is today, although one man said that the only explanation of my work was the use of logarithms.

One does not have to go to the wilds of Australia or to the jungles of Africa to see peculiar people. There are many of them in the cities who do not know they are peculiar, and many more out in the rural districts who don't care if they are. I probably met more peculiar people than anyone else in the world, and right here in glorious small town U.S.A.

The oddest I ever met were at a little settlement in the hill country of a southern state. It was a collection of a few houses without a name, and it was not on any map. I found it by chance while scouting about the country, looking for a place to show in. This was in later years when I had an auto and house trailer. Besides the few hovels used as dwellings, there was the usual small store and tumble down building in which to give a show.   The whole community looked like a good place for a murder.   It was nearly nightfall and I decided to remain there all night and move along in the morning, if I were still alive.

As there was no show that night I had a chance to talk to the natives who loafed in the store. I learned that the store was owned by Miss Pansy, that she was 26, and that her husband was over 75 years of age. Miss Pansy had started her store on a cash capital of seven dollars. She had quite a stock for a small store and I wondered how she could do it with seven dollars, until I found out that she also bootlegged whiskey and put the profit from that business into groceries for the store. She had been convicted of violating the liquor law and a fine was assessed against her. This she was unable to pay. The authorities paroled her so that she could harvest a cotton crop on her small farm and thus obtain money with which to pay the fine. Miss Pansy was ignorant, filthy, and profane; but like a dirty white dog, she was really good looking when she was scrubbed clean and fumigated. She carried a pistol and she feared no one. Several times she sent me cooked food at mealtimes. This was not fit to eat. I wrapped it in a piece of paper and took it down the road and threw it among the thick honeysuckle vines.

While Miss Pansy punctuated her conversation with oaths, dipped snuff and was as tough as they made them, she became terrified at the approach of a storm. At the first darkening of the skies she would gather everyone around her, kneel, and supplicate the good Lord in a fervent and well worded prayer for protection from the storm. This prayer was always granted while I was there. As soon as the storm was over, she would resume her profanity and forget to give thanks for her protection.

The surrounding country was swampy and harbored numerous distillers of illicit whiskey, along with other shady characters. There was a paroled murderer, a jail escapee and many other people who should have been locked up. During the evening a number of the men engaged in a drunken brawl, and one of them was knocked unconscious. They dragged him under my house trailer, where he remained for several hours before gaining consciousness. All of this convinced me I had better make a quick getaway. My engine would not start. Investigation revealed that some hard to get repairs were needed. I had to send to the city for these and I had to stay among those hard boiled nuts for ten days. Tough as they were, they liked me and my show and were as friendly as it was possible for people of their nature and disposition to be.

There was one tough character who, when intoxicated, would start trouble with anyone he might contact. The sitters in the store warned me against him and told me to be on my guard, and they also said that they would be ready to help me in case I needed it. An old Negro said, "Mistah Gus, do you all see this black fist?" "Yes," I said. "Well, when dis black fist hits a white man in de eye he gits a black eye fo' sure, an' certain an dats jest what he'll get iffen he stahts picken on you all." Miss Pansy said, "Iffen he stahts messin' with you'all, he'll git a hunk o'lead outen mah gun." With the backing of these two prominent citizens, I had no fear of the tough guy. In fact, he never got tough.

I showed at this spot after my wife had died, and some of the natives must have thought that I was a good matrimonial catch. One day a man and a girl came to my trailer house to visit me. After some conversation, the man said, "Mister Gus, if you wanted her, Mildred would marry up with you." I just laughed and said, "What does Mildred want with an old bloke like me?" "She likes you pretty well," he said. I eased them away as diplomatically as I could. For the benefit of those interested, I might explain that Mildred was twelve years of age and that her father was drunk. Later I learned that her younger sister, about ten, was going to marry a man of seventy, a brother of Miss Pansy's husband. At the same time, a man told me that if I wanted to get married he knew of a good chance for me. He said he was acquainted with a widow, "widder woman," he termed her, who had a fine farm and money in the bank and who was anxious to get married again. He had appointed himself a committee of one to get her married, and to me. He insisted I go with him to her farm to make her acquaintance. By one pretext or another I managed to evade the trip to see the lady. I made inquiries, however, and found out that the "widder" looked and was built like a huge hippopotamus, that her bank account was not more than a few hundred dollars, and that her fine farm was in a river bottom. Every spring when the river flooded it washed away everything that was not spiked down. As an added attraction, she chewed tobacco. As soon as I received the repair parts for my car, I left these wonderful people with a promise to visit them sometime — a promise I haven't kept.

Country people had peculiar names. Most of them were Biblical names, or names such as those, contorted. Sometimes they called each other by names not fit to print. There was one name which seemed to fit all of them, though, and that name was rubes. Just what a rube is, is a matter of opinion. Rubes living in New York consider those living in a smaller town like Duluth to be rubes. Rube residents of Duluth (if any) consider those living in Kokomo to be rubes. The rubes of Kokomo think villagers are rubes, and the villagers speak of farmers as rubes. One farmer who had just returned from a visit to a big city concluded the puzzle by saying, "They's more rubes in a big town than I thot wuz in the hull world." Maybe he was right. One thing is certain, the larger the city, the more inhabitants there are in it who are qualified to become city rubes, which are the most disgusting sort of all. I sometimes wonder if we are all rubes but do not realize it. I did not find the word rube in the dictionary which I consulted, however, so perhaps there is no such animal.

Whether they were rubes or not, all small towns had a few outstanding citizens of rank, meaning they were so rank they should have been standing out in the rain in order to get a bath. Citizen Number 1 was the mayor. If he happened to be an old man suffering with indigestion and rheumatism, he was hard to do business with. The ideal mayor was the village doctor, acting in that capacity. He, of course, would be an educated man and would be easy to deal with. There was not much for a small town mayor to do but to take the blame for everything that went wrong and fail to get credit when things went right.

Next in line came the town marshall. He was the village police department, and he was not timid about assuming that attitude, especially before strangers. He did not make much of an impression on the rougher element in the village, who would give him a beating when he became too arrogant or overbearing. Occasionally, there was a mail order detective, one who had taken a correspondence course in police work. In that case he would wear an honest to goodness, nickel plated star, lettered "Police." Also, he would carry a billy and a revolver. If in addition to all this he wore a cheap, blue uniform with brass buttons, he was quite an adornment to the village streets and the giddy country girls would fall in love with him. About the first words one of these keepers of the peace would utter, when he found out that I had a show, were,

"Does I and my family get in the show free?" If I wanted police protection while I was in the town I was compelled to answer, "Yes, you do." All town marshals had one common peculiarity. That was their ability to vanish completely when their services were required.

As a rule, town marshals were a dumb set, but a few of them were clever in their own peculiar way. One had an ingenious method which he used for getting rid of undesirable out of towners, who came to town to become intoxicated and made themselves generally obnoxious. He would arrest them, put them in a jail cell, and pretend to lock them in. He fastened the door just enough to keep it closed. As soon as the marshall was gone, the prisoners would discover the unlocked door, make their escape, and leave town in a hurry. With the possibility of two charges — drunk and disorderly conduct and jail breaking — being brought against them, they remained away from that town for a long time. This was just what the marshall wanted, and this was the easiest way to do it

An original way of settling a dispute was used by a marshall in a small western village. There was a billboard in front of the jail. Two rival bill posters who wanted to paste a bill on it at the same time became involved in a fistfight. The marshall arrived on the scene and settled the argument in a very satisfactory manner. Instead of arresting the bill posters and bringing a charge of disorderly conduct against them, he put the billboard in a jail cell and locked the door so that neither of them could use it. Some diplomat.

While the average small town marshall was not very dependable, I encountered one who was overly zealous in attending to his duties. While the show was in progress, he could tell by the red tinge in the sky that there was a farm building burning a few miles out in the country. He wanted to alert the audience, but he went about it in a wrong way. He opened the hall door and said in a loud voice, "Don't be alarmed, but there is a fire!" What he intended to say was, "Don't be alarmed, there is a fire two miles out in the country." When the people in the audience heard the word "fire," they made a quick scramble for the exit, and in less than a minute the hall was empty. As soon as they discovered that the fire was at a distance, the people filed nicely back into the hall and the show went on as all good shows are supposed to do.

I had another experience with an unusually ambitious limb of the law. I was exhibiting in a town hall. During the performance, the marshall paraded up and down the aisles, watching the audience, which was very quiet. In fact, it was so quiet that I thought that I had not made much of an impression with my performance. After the show I asked the marshall how they liked it. His answer was, "Pretty tolerable," which sounded as though it could be tolerated but which meant "Pretty good." I ventured to remark, "They were very quiet, nobody laughed or clapped their hands." "They know'd better'n to make any disturbing noise like that 'cause they know'd iffen they did I'd make them git out of the opery," he answered.

Probably the most efficient small town marshall in the world policed a place I showed many years ago. There was a trio of rough brothers who would come to town in the evening, get drunk, and start a fight with anyone they happened to meet. If the marshall interfered, they would beat him up. For a long time, nobody wanted the police job in that town, as everyone was afraid of the hoodlums. Finally, a young Irishman offered to take the job. He was invested with police authority and was given a star. He did not want a revolver, but he did carry a heavy hickory cane which was so large at the top that it deserved the title of club or shillalah. The first night he was on duty, the bad boys attacked him. He hit each of them on the head with his club cane, cracking their skulls and killing them. No mention of the affair was made in the local newspapers. The officer was not taken into court. The whole affair was ignored, and law and order prevailed. When I played the same town twenty years later they still had the same town marshall, who still carried the same hickory cane, and law and order still prevailed.

The doctor was next in line among the town's representatives, although according to all standards he should be placed first, and "Saint" would have been a more appropriate title. He was the man who would arise from a warm bed on a cold winter night and walk to a home to treat a suffering person. He furnished the medicine and charged as little as a dollar, which in many instances he was unable to collect. He did not refer one to a high priced specialist because there were none, although they are in full force now (for mutual protection they congregate in tall office buildings — it seems that the higher the building they operate in,the higher their consultation fee). Generally he was the only educated man in town. Most doctors were qualified as M.D.'s, but anyone could style himself doctor and practice medicine, as all laws were lax anyway back in the '80s and '90s. Those places without a doctor had to depend on the dubious experience of old women and their epsom salts and mustard plasters. In their crude way, these women were fairly competent. At least they were better than no doctor at all.

I met an odd character in one of the small towns in which I was showing. I went into the town looking for a piece of ground, usually termed a lot, to pitch my tent. As I was a total stranger in the place, I had to make some inquiries. The first person I encountered was a man seated on a chair on a small platform or uncovered porch, in front of a dilapidated house. He was seated at the center of the platform, and in a semicircle in front of him there were squirts of tobacco juice. There would have been a complete circle, but he could not squirt sideways or behind himself. He was reading from a few leaflets he held in his hand, which I later I learned were ready made religious sermons that he was studying. When I explained my business to him, he offered to find a lot for me. He took me to the edge of town, showed me a piece of ground, and then took me to its owner, who rented it to me for a week. Then he told me that he was the local preacher, and that he had three other churches in nearby towns. He had a team of spotted ponies, and he took me to those three places and secured lots for me and places to board — all of this without charge. When Sunday

49

morning came, we went to his service. The church was filled to the doors. He was not an educated or ordained minister. He was one of those self-appointed preachers. His sermon was convincing, if not eloquent. His grammar was bad. He used the phrases "have saw," "have went", and "ain't no sech thing." His listeners gave good attention, and I believe his sermons were as good as those of the most highly educated clergyman. He took up no collection. I was told that his other three churches were always filled to capacity, and that before he took charge of them, there was no attendance at all.

The storekeeper must not be overlooked. In case you do not know it, he was the man with dirty hands who kept the store and handled all of the bulk food. Nothing was ever in any kind of order and nothing was clean. Food was exposed in open containers and millions of flies ate sugar off the raisins and other foods. Crackers, sugar, prunes, and other foods came in barrels instead of in the fancy, sanitary containers of the present day. The barrels were not screened and insects had a perpetual holiday. Men with dirty overalls would sit on the edges of the barrels. I often wonder if that was what made mother's cooking so good. The backwoods legislators would meet here in cold weather, gathering around the stove to regulate the affairs of the home and nation in true democratic fashion. While arguing, they decorated the stove with tobacco spit, despite the sign above it reading, "Spit in the stove, not at it." This must have been a hereditary habit, as I cannot conceive of anyone wishing to adopt it voluntarily. The country merchant gave no thrift stamps, but plug tobacco had tin tags attached which could be exchanged for merchandise. And he did give an extra item on a dozen or give a child a stick of peppermint candy.

Anyone who owned a dirty mug and lather brush, a dull razor, a greasy comb, and a pair of rusty scissors could pose as a barber and open shop, proceeding unmolested. He could use the same lather, mug and brush for as many customers as he desired without giving sanitation or cleanliness a thought. Many men cut each other's hair. A favorite place during the summertime was in the backyard under a shade tree and, if possible, near the pig sty. Of course, the resultant haircuts somewhat resembled a disgruntled porcupine, but they were haircuts nevertheless. Their cost was nil. If there happened to be a drugstore, it was always just that. Lawn mowers and tractors had not been invented at that time, and so were not stocked. All drugstores specialized in laxatives and morphine. There was always plenty of the latter available at very low cost.

Especially memorable were the backhouses. In the city they were called bathrooms. They were standard equipment in all homesteads. They were freezing in the winter and torrid in the summer, when they harbored flies, wasps, and spiders. While they were generally obnoxious, they seemed to be a necessary evil.

The inside walls were embellished with an objectionable style of American literature. It was a choice collection of vulgar or immoral poetry and sayings. Some of these were quite witty and entertaining to a person with a depraved and rotten mind. If I had recorded all of the mural jokes and verses I read in these places during my sixty years of rural ramblings, I could publish a good-sized book which would be the world's best seller but for the fact that the post office department would bar it from the mails. In order to discourage this style of literature, one man papered the inside of his outdoor bathroom with religious pictures. Girls and women always visited the backhouse in pairs. No one knew why, though it was generally supposed that they went there to tell jokes, there being no beauty parlors to use at that time. Maybe it was to exchange secrets or to rave over their beaus. They always occupied the place for an unreasonably long time. When someone lingered too long, one landlord would go out on the back porch and play the "Star Spangled Banner" on his cornet. That made them stand up. One woman solved the cold weather problem nicely; she had a large ring of quilted cloth which she warmed and took with her to place on the seat. To prevent the ring from becoming prematurely cold she had to run to her goal. With the black ring in one hand and an old newspaper in the other, she was a pleasing diversion to the neighbors.

Some of these booths were quite ornate according to the rural standards of that day. They were trimmed with ginger-bread work and painted with all colors in or out of the rainbow. The door would have a heart or crescent- shaped opening near the top, high enough so no one could look in. Old maids (now extinct) were very particular about having these openings very high. In some of them would be a cowbell. This the sitter could ring when he (or she) heard someone approaching. These necessary accessories to life, liberty and the pursuit of happiness were located as far from the residence as possible— a long, healthy walk in cold winter weather. They seemed to always be near the well.

Backhouses were sometimes used for purposes other than their legitimate one. I wanted to go in one once, and found that a trio of little girls had preempted it to use for a play party. For a wonder, the table was clean, and fortunately they had mud pies for food. When a sextet of hens took to roosting in one all night, well, you can imagine. Having no other place to keep his vegetables, the owner of a hotel used his little house to store potatoes, onions, cabbages, and carrots. If it were not for the odor, one might think he was in a vegetable market. It is well known that some vegetables absorb odors from the atmosphere. I was thankful that I only used the little house there and ate at another hotel.

I know of a man who used his little house to torment his next door neighbor, with whom he was on unfriendly terms. He had no more use for his diminutive habitation, as he had installed a private water works in his home and had a regularly appointed bathroom. He moved the discarded out-house as near to his back door and as close to his neighbor's kitchen as he could. This, of course, infuriated the neighbor, and that was just what the other man expected and wanted. The village was not incorporated, so there was no legal recourse for him there. Mad as a wet hen, he drove all the way to the county seat to complain to the sheriff. That gentleman drove to the village to notify the supposed offender that he must remove the offensive building. "What offensive building?" he said. "Can't a man put his tool house anywhere he wants to on his property?" With that, he opened the door and showed the interior, minus the seat and excavation but filled with a lawn mower, hoe, spade, and other garden tools. The sheriff became vexed and severely berated the neighbor.

On one occasion I had obtained permission to set up my tent at the end of an unused street. The street was wide enough to accommodate the show tent proper, but I needed more space for the guy ropes and stakes. Beside the street there was a lawn with shade trees which would be a fine place for the smaller tent. Also, there was a drilled well which would furnish pure drinking water. I went to the house to ask permission to use the lawn. The lady who responded to my knock looked at me rather suspiciously. After stating my request, her look became militant. She hesitated somewhat, but finally said, "Yes, you can drive your stakes on our lawn, you can put your little tent under our shade trees, and you can get water from our well; but there is one thing you can't do. You can't use our little house. Them last show people what was here fixed our little house and we don't want no more show people to use it." She did not say how the little house had been fixed and I did not want to question her. We used her lawn, shade trees and well. We spent an enjoyable and profitable week there, regardless of the fact that we did not have the use of her little house.

The inevitable livery stable could easily be located by its odor. Usually there was a bench or two at the front, occupied in warm weather by town loafers who whittled, made remarks about passing women, spit tobacco juice on the sidewalk, and ran or criticized the government. At the livery, one could nearly always rent a rheumatic horse and a wrecked buggy for a dollar a day. The horse almost always lived long enough to make the round trip. The livery stable was also headquarters for the village bottle brigade. Members carried a bottle for periodic drinks in the privacy of the stalls and threw the empty bottles on the manure pile behind the barn. When the farmers came to haul the manure away to be used as fertilizer, they had to sort out the bottles. One enterprising youth collected the bottles and sold them to a junk man. He has probably developed into one of our industrial leaders.

Fire fighting equipment in small towns was never very satisfactory. It consisted mostly of a hand-operated pump, powered by eight volunteer firemen. If the pump had a tank for carrying a supply of water, it was called a tub. The pump would throw a stream of water a reasonable distance, but a good supply of water was not always available. As soon as the supply from nearby wells was exhausted, there was nothing the firemen could do but watch the fire. The pump was mounted on wheels and could be drawn by man or horsepower. When the fire alarm sounded, the first man to arrive at the firehouse with a team of horses could haul the pump to the scene of the fire and be paid two dollars for his services. On one occasion two men arrived at the same time. A quarrel ensued, each man insisting he had the right to haul the pump. By the time they had the argument settled, the fire had progressed so far it could not be extinguished.

In another little town the firemen decided to purchase more modern fire fighting equipment. They bought a bright red truck fitted with ladders, axes, buckets, and chemical extinguishers. The outfit was the finest in that section of the country. It was dedicated on the afternoon of the Fourth of July. It was placed in front of the firehouse and bedecked with flags and flowers for the spectators to admire. After an invocation by the minister, a song by the children, and a speech by the mayor, the truck was to have been backed into the shelter of the fire house. All went well until the truck could not move through a door six inches too narrow for its passage. So the pride of the village had to remain outside at the mercy of the elements and small boys until the door could be enlarged.

Schools were mostly of the one room kind. There were not as many high schools and colleges then as there are now.

If we wanted a knowledge of vulgar words and wanted to learn to curse and swear, we had to be satisfied with grade school standards. If we did not like that kind of knowledge, we did not have to go to school, there being no compulsion. Teachers were elderly women with severe and forbidding countenance. Physical punishment was the rule of the day, and most children did not love their teachers. Anyone could teach in those small town schools. No special education was needed. A little girl with whose family we were boarding came home from school with a fine report card. She rated 100 percent in most studies, with a few in which she had 98. Her mother was pleased and said, "That's fine, Jennie, but wouldn't it be nice if you could get 100 in everything?" The girl quickly answered, "I couldn't do that, mother. Such a good teacher we ain't got."

Election day was always welcome in the village. It was a good reason for having a holiday and not having to work. Nearly everybody voted, but not many of them could tell why they voted the way they did. Some of them voted the way their fathers and grandfathers voted, thereby admitting that they did not have brains enough to make their own decisions. Some voted in a particular way because a lot of others voted that way. Some voted according to the editorials in the county newspaper. Some voted under the influence of a generous amount of free beer and whiskey. A few listened attentively to the arguments of paid speakers of all political parties and then tried to decide which one told the least number of lies. When they concluded that there was no such thing as a "least" number of lies, they decided not to vote. Women were immune to criticism such as this, because they could not vote in those days.

Highways were chiefly a long strip of earth bordered on each side by weeds and a fence, generally of the rail variety. The middle was ornamented with deep ruts cut by wagon wheels during wet weather, when most roads were impassable. During dry weather the mud became an impalpable powder. In the winter time they were too icy or too deep with snow. The country roads were always bad. They were not numbered or named. Occasionally there was a guidepost with weather worn and indistinguishable letters. Only animals knew where they were going. When returning home on a long drive, I would depend on the horse to turn at the proper corner. A mariner might travel around easily, as he could guide himself by the sun. In the prairie country, one could see the high grain elevator at the railroad station six miles or so away and head for that. The main and side roads looked alike. The main roads were not distinguished by a generous sprinkling of empty beer cans because beer was not canned at that time; it was sold by the bucketful for a nickel.

Little towns had railroads, but this did not mean that they had train service. Some trains stopped only on signal, and most of them did not stop at all. Trains were almost always late. Those which did stop were mixed passenger and freight trains which carried passengers in the caboose. They would stop for as long as half an hour, loading and unloading freight, switching back and forth, and punishing passengers with bumps every time they moved. The passengers were short distance travellers. No one could have survived a long journey. The regular passenger trains were a vast improvement over the mixed or accommodation trains. These moved at a speed of twenty miles per hour, too fast for safety. Women would scream and become hysterical. Always there was a crying baby aboard. Most engines were coal burners, though some burned wood. The coaches were not ventilated. Windows stuck, and the railroad employees did not furnish crowbars to open them. When it was possible to open them, coal smoke and cinders blew in to add to the miseries of poor ventilation. When the train was started by a violent jerk from the engine, the passengers were thrown against the seat backs. Almost the same performance was repeated in reverse when the train came to a sudden stop, the difference being that the riders were thrown against the back of the seat ahead of them. Everyone laughed and thought it was fun, especially the children.

To many of the natives, the arrival of the train was an

event of importance. All of the unemployed bums of the village were there to watch it come and go. Travelling salesmen who visited the town took orders for merchandise and as a sideline picked up the town girls who were on the platform waiting to be picked up. These were considered bad, very bad girls. Good girls would not do anything like that. They did other bad things, but were smart enough not to get caught at it.

Few things occurred to mar the equanimity of affairs in the little places. An accidental death or suicide affected everyone, as everybody was acquainted with everybody else. I happened to be unfortunate enough to be showing in a town where a resident took his life. Let's name him John. John was the owner of one of the few really good country hotels I ever came in contact with. He had the reputation of serving the best meals in that section of the country. With an incubator he hatched eggs so that he had a young chicken to serve for dinner every day in the year. Travellers would try to go to John's whenever they were in his locality. They passed up expensive hotels in the cities to be able to dine at John's. But John had a different opinion of himself. He thought his meals were inferior and his hotel service unsatisfactory. He also imagined that everyone else felt the same way. If two people were conversing in an undertone, John was sure they were criticizing his hotel service. If someone told him his dinner was excellent, he thought they were being sarcastic or did not mean what they said. These things preyed on his mind until he became so despondent that he took his life by going into a culvert under a train track and swallowing carbolic acid.

Now a series of unfortunate events occurred. First, John was a member of the Catholic church. That church did not allow a suicide to be buried in its cemetery. Relatives tried to obtain a plot of burial ground in the Protestant cemetery. This was refused them, with the information that the Protestants did not want any Catholic rubbish in their cemetery regardless of church rules. Then an effort was made to get the Catholic sexton to dig a grave in his cemetery, regardless of church rules. He refused. The Protestant sexton was induced to dig a grave in the Catholic cemetery. When his work was about half done, the Catholic priest ordered him off of the grounds. When he refused to go, the priest attacked him with a spade. Then he went. All of this took about four days, and John remained a corpse without a burial place. Next someone started the report that John could be buried in the Catholic cemetery if the grave was under the fence with the head on the outside; the legs and lower body could be on the inside of the fence. It took a day to disprove this falsehood. This was too much for the priest, who left town for more peaceful surroundings. As all of the people were in too much of a turmoil to attend a show, I decided to move to another town myself. On the way to the railway station I passed the place where John's body lay. Through the open door I could see a number of women kneeling and reciting the rosary. I never found out how it all ended, but my advice to would-be suicides is don't do it in a small town. Wakes were affairs where men stayed up all night to keep company with the corpse, mourn, and have a good time. Many wakes of the 1880's were hilarious affairs, especially if a sufficient amount of liquor was furnished to drown the sorrows and elevate the spirits. When the watchers were sufficiently liquored up almost anything could happen. Frequently it did. At a wake where candles were burned on the coffin, the befuddled mourners did not notice when the candles burned to the bottom and set the coffin afire. At another wake the men became so irresponsible that they took the body from the coffin, stood it in a corner of the room, put a pipe in its mouth, and made insulting accusations to it daring it to talk back. Most wakes had a fist fight or two before the party broke up in the morning. This extinct custom was always a pleasing diversion to those who liked whiskey. The modern funeral home is a big improvement over the wakes. Now friends can meet to renew old friendships, have an informal party and engage in the latest gossip – no liquor, no drunks, no fights. Just a nice, pleasant, informal party.

Recreational facilities were limited. A second-class show coming to town was a major attraction. Special holidays were anticipated with enthusiasm. The Fourth of July celebration, with its attendant burns, inferior ice creams and consequent bellyaches, was a great event. The Sunday School picnic took place, rain or shine. Most of the time it rained. Auction sales were a big attraction, because a lunch consisting of weak coffee, greasy doughnuts, dirty crackers, and cheese was served free. There was also croquet and horseshoe pitching to waste time on. Little boys had slingshots and amused themselves by breaking windows or killing birds, or both. Little girls, being more decorous, made mud pies and played house. During the winter season there were spelling bees, public debates, corn huskings, quilting parties, sewing circles, and other excuses for congregating and having a goose gabble. Hayrides were popular.

Young men and women had home parties featuring kissing games. Young men frequented pool halls where they could play cards unobserved in a back room. Card playing was considered a devil's pastime by some. After supper (country people had dinner at noon), young children went to bed. Older children did their homework if forced to do so. Sometimes company came, and popped corn, apples and cider would be served. Grandpa sat by the stove and smoked his smelly pipe, while Grandma just sat. Frequently they both just sat. Adults whose vision was good read the usual almanacs, such as "Old Farmer," "Dr. Jaynes," and "Hostetters." Nights when everyone remained at home, they had their regular family arguments. The day was concluded with family prayers.

MR. and MRS. RAPP
ENTERTAINERS

IN A MELANGE OF
MUSIC—MIRTH—MYSTERY

CLEVER MAGICAL
MANIPULATIONS

SPIRITUALISTIC
MYSTERIES
EXPOSED

EXTRAORDINARY
THOUGHT
READING TESTS

MUSICAL
NOVELTIES

SWEET TONED
GLASSES

STEEL HARP,
XYLOPHONE,
MUSICAL BOWLS,
ETC.

STRICTLY MORAL
OFFENDS NONE
PLEASES ALL

The entertainments are strictly high grade and given to satisfy the desires of the public for a refined form of amusement which shall be entertaining and instructive at the same time.

CHAPTER FOUR

BOOKING SMALL TOWNS

To book these places for a show was about as difficult a piece of work as trying to book a theatre in metropolitan cities. For a start, a place had to be located. As they were hardly ever on a map, I had to ask a native where to find one. If I happened to inquire of a group of natives, each would tell me a different place that would be sure to be suitable. After I had decided on a place I would have to find out about the best wagon road to use to get there. Each person would have a different route to suggest. As I had to drive to the town and return in time for the evening show, I had to arise at 6 a.m., hire a horse and buggy at the livery stable or from a farmer, and drive to a spot ten miles away. This was in the days before the R.F.D. service, and I also had to drive six miles once a week to the nearest post office to get my mail. Sometimes I was fortunate enough to obtain a good horse, and many times I was unfortunate enough to get a bad one. During the winter season I had to start out before daylight, regardless of zero temperature, rain, wind, sleet, or snow.

Most livery horses were old and unfit for such strenuous work. I was not fit for such work either, but I did not realize it at the time. When I arrived at my destination the first thing to be done was to put the horse in the barn and have him fed. I had to watch the horse eat, because some unscrupulous livery men would put the horse in the stall without feeding him but would charge and collect the price of his meal. So I always watched and saw that the corn was put in the manger. Later I found out that as soon as I was gone, the cheap robber would sometimes take the grain away. So I had to remain with the horse until he was through eating if I wanted to be sure that he had a meal which would give him strength to endure the return trip. Once I remained with the horse so long that dinner at the hotel was over and I missed mine. I went to the store and bought five cents worth of crackers and cheese combined for my lunch. If I had eaten at the country hotel the dinner would have cost me fifteen cents, so I saved a dime, which was a considerable amount of money at that time.

To book even as small a one-horse show such as mine was no easy matter. I had to know everything there was to know about show business. I had to know at which seasons of the year to go to certain sections. The tobacco growing sections were profitable only at the time tobacco was being sold. To go there at any other time would be to find most of the tobacco farmers penniless, with no money to spend for shows. However, as soon as the tobacco sales started, my hall would be filled every evening. The same was true of the strawberry country, the potato country, and cotton sections. General farming country was good after harvesting and threshing or when grain was being sold. Dairy country, where the farmers received a check every fortnight for their cream, was good at almost any time. I had to be among the Indians when they received their allowance from the government. In the spring of the year, when farmers were unusually busy because of the planting season, I had to go to larger places where I could draw an audience from the town people and did not have to depend on the farmers for patronage. I also had to find out if there might be some other activity in progress, such as a revival meeting, which might attract a crowd. If there were, I had to skip the town and play it at some later date.

I had to stay out of places where the people were largely of a religious belief that did not countenance shows. If there was a case of smallpox twenty miles away, I would not be able to attract a crowd. During the spring thawing season, I had to stay out of mud country which did not have paved roads. If the small town had just had a number of shows, another one would not be a profitable venture. If the last show did not give satisfaction, the town would be a good place to stay away from. When I did find a place with no objectionable features, I might go there and encounter a week of bad weather which would be as big a knock as anything. The small show business was a gamble. The only difference between me and a professional gambler was that the latter did his gamblings in an easy way at a card or roulette table, while I did mine the hard way, by working from twelve to fifteen hours a day.

After checking a town according to the above arbitrary formulae, there were other things which had to be taken into consideration. A good stock of merchandise in the store would suggest that it did a good business, which in turn meant that the farmers in the surrounding country were prosperous. If the store was a long distance from other trade centers, it would have a good trade, which was always a good indication of good show business. If the town people sponsored a lyceum attraction, it was almost a certainty that a road show could not attract a crowd. The local people had to pay a high price to get the lyceum entertainers to come to a small town. In many instances, it was more than they were worth. This gave them the impression that the lyceum artists were of unusual merit and far above the common actor or little showman in ability and social standing. Therefore, they could not lower themselves or their dignity by showing approval of an ordinary show. They sometimes went so far as to boycott an independent show. The city lyceum attractions were meritorious and of a high quality, but those that came to the villages were inferior. They did not give the audience the satisfaction that my little ten-cent show did.

Another indication of a profitable spot was a saloon. A saloon town was always good for me. It was probably because the persons who patronized saloons were good spenders and would be equally generous with their money in spending it at shows. Even though a town resident told me the place was not a good show town I would not always believe him that such was the case. Such an individual might have some personal reason for not wanting a show. He might be a pool hall operator, in which case a show would attract some of his customers. He might have a large family and feel that he could not afford to treat them to a show. A clergyman might tell me that the place was not a good show town because my presence might reduce the size of his Sunday morning collection. Or there might be many other reasons. I could not accept any one person's word when he told me a place would not be profitable. One hotel clerk said he felt sorry for shows that came to his town, because in over twenty years the largest crowd that ever assembled in the hall was seventeen people. As I could find no other place to go to, I booked the town. I showed a week to good business and on the last night had a capacity crowd of over 400 persons, which was a large crowd for a small show.

One of the best indications of a desirable show town was good patronage at the store by the surrounding farmers. I had a very primitive method for obtaining information about this. Farmers came to town via horse and buggy or horse and wagon. They tied their horses to the convenient hitching posts located along the edge of the sidewalk. Horses remaining at one place for any length of time always left evidence on the ground. As the streets were never cleaned, the amount of horse evidence on the ground would be indicative of the number of farmers who came to town to trade.

Next on the agendum was to locate the hall manager. He was liable to be found anywhere. He might be a merchant. He might be a clergyman, a saloon keeper or a common bum. Some of the hall managers were nice people to meet and some were so ignorant and ill mannered as to make me wish that I had adopted sewer cleaning instead of entertaining as a means of livelihood. They were always hard to transact business with because most of them were unreliable characters and they imagined that everyone else was of the same breed of cattle. Principally, they were afraid that I would fail to pay the hall rent. This had happened in the case of other shows. Some managers wanted me to load them up on liquor before they would talk business. I would quickly decide that

I did not want the hall or the town. When I told one swarthy looking brigand that I did not drink, he gave me a contemptuous look and said, "Well, I do. Look down my throat, do you see anything?" I admitted that I could not see anything. "You ought to," he said, "because three farms went down that way." Once, when I thought I was being asked too much rent by the hall owner, I told him I would have to go see about another hall which I knew was located at the other end of town. He just smiled and said, "You can have that one at the same price; I own that one, too." The backwoods theatrical magnates liked to question the value of the show. To give you an idea of what some persons thought of a show, here is a short conversation I had. The native said, "Say, we got a feller in this town who oughta be in your show." Not knowing what else to say, I asked, "What can he do?" "Do?" replied the other. "Why, that's jest it, he can't do nothing. He ain't fittin' fer nothin' but a show." Said one, "We ain't had nothin' but rotten shows as long as I kin remember. Is your show rotten?" I retorted in no mild manner, saying, "I think you will find my show to be as good as your dirty hall or this punk little town." He shot back, "Your show's gotta be better'n the oprey or the town, 'cause we got the worst oprey and the nastiest town this side o' hell and your shows gotta be better'n them or you better git out o' town."

An equally pleasant gentleman insisted on telling me what a bad specimen of humanity he was. He lived on a farm just outside of the village. He told me about a farmer who went to a neighboring farmer and borrowed his gun and dog to go hunting with, early the next morning. In the middle of the night, when the neighbor was without a warning dog or gun, the borrower raided his chicken coop and stole all of his chickens. He said to me, "Everybody thought I was the thief; it was me all right, but hell, they can't do nothin' about it cause they ain't got no proof agin' me." These are just samples of the high-class citizenry I was forced to associate with.

An old German managed the hall at one place. He spoke with an accent. "Is this town composed of foreigners?" I asked.

"No,dere is only one foreigner here, he is a Norwegian. All the rest is Germans." "Can everyone speak English?" I asked. "Yes," he answered, "dey can all talk English, but ve got one feller here vat can talk dree laguandges: English, German and Vendrolykism." "Do you have a hall or opera house?" I asked. "Yes, ve got a obrey house," he replied. I wanted to know, "Is it fully equipped?" "'Vell," he said, "it's got seeds for the beoble to sit on, a stage to act on, dere is lights for yours feed, rooms to change dresses in. Ve got a parlor, sidding room, kitchen, timber, and a penitentiary, ve got curtains vat roll up and down." "Where is the hall?" I asked. "Oud in the country, ve got to clean it oud first, it's got chickens in it now." As the place did not look good to me, I continued my questioning: "Does this place have a church?" "No," he replied. "Does it have a post office?" "No," he replied. "Does it have a school?" "No," he replied. "Well," I said, "no church, no post office, no school; tell me, just what is this town good for?" "Vell, mister," said the German, "dis town ain't good for noddings but shows." So I booked the town and played the place for a week to turn away business. The old German was right, the town was "good for noddings but shows."

That the town hall manager was sometimes engaged in other occupations was forced on me in a very realistic manner. One night after the show we went to the hotel and to bed. At about two A.M., my wife awoke with a severe headache. The only headache remedy we had was at the hall. I dressed and groped my way down the unlighted village street with the aid of a coal oil lantern. As my wife was afraid to remain alone in the hotel at that time of night, she went along. When we entered the hall we saw what looked like some clothes or a man asleep on a string of chairs. Closer inspection revealed that it was a man. I thought it was some drunk who had failed to leave the hall when the show was over and was sleeping on the chairs. Bringing the lantern closer, we discovered that it was not only a man but a dead one with his throat cut. My wife shrieked and we ran from the hall and back to the hotel as fast as we could. My wife had forgotten her headache. In the morning when I went to the hall, the body was gone. The explanation was very simple. The hall manager was also the local coroner. A man had committed suicide out in the country. The coroner had brought the body to town after the show was over, and having no better place he put it in the hall until morning, when he took it to the county seat. After that I kept a supply of headache remedy in the hotel.

Nearly every small town or village had some kind of an excuse of a building to hold public or community gatherings, such as political meetings, elections, dances, and religious services. No matter how old, dirty, dilapidated, and inconvenient these buildings were, they were always dignified by the name of Opera House, pronounced by the natives "Oprey House," or just plain "Oprey." Fortunately, the roofs of some of these antiquated structures did not leak. When there was no regular hall or "oprey," I had to improvise one. I could take any room which was of sufficient size and convert it into a usable little theatre. I carried curtains and other equipment for doing this. Sometimes when they were completed they looked like a joke (a bad one), but they were nearly always money making affairs. Once I showed over a blacksmith shop, and at another time, over a livery stable. Both were good money makers, although the livery stable was slightly off standard as to odor. One hall was upstairs over a store. A rickety wooden stairway on the outside of the building was the only way of entering or leaving the hall. Show patrons arrived a few at a time, so the stairway was not overloaded before the show. When it was over, however, they would have all crowded onto it at one time, and it would have broken down. So I stationed someone at the top of the stairs who would limit the number of descending persons to a few at a time. There were no fire laws at that time or place, or I would not have been allowed to use the building.

To heat the halls a stove with a broken grate or no grate at all was frequently used. When someone had a stove which was definitely out of service, it could always find a welcome resting place in the town oprey. The stove was always put at the front of the hall, near the entrance so that the performers on the stage did not receive any benefit from its heat. Generally the hall manager did not furnish a sufficient amount of fuel. In cold weather, the first comers would crowd around the stove and manage to keep one side warm, while those away from it were cold on both sides. If the men around the stove could find a coal bucket to spit tobacco juice in, they seemed to be supremely happy. Sometimes the hall was warm, but the stage was cold. When the curtain went up, the heavy cold air would roll out over the front of the stage like a waterfall and chill the occupants of the front rows. Some wise old ladies brought hot bricks to put under their feet to keep them warm. Occasionally the stage was so cold that the water used for tricks froze during the show. The dressing rooms were always cold. Once I sent word to the janitor to fire up, as we were freezing. In a few minutes he came backstage and handed us two smelly horse blankets, saying, "Wrap these around you and you'll keep warm." As there was a law against murder, I did not commit that crime.

If the so called stage happened to have scenery, it was such in name only. It was usually crude attempts made by high school boys for their home talent plays. Occasionally there was a scanty assortment of wings and a roller curtain which was invariably out of order. Either the pull ropes were old and broken, or they would stick in the pulleys when the curtain was halfway up. This always provoked much laughter, hoots and howls from the assembled customers, especially the smaller ones. In order to keep the small town stage hands (if any) from prying into my magical secrets, I always dispensed with their services and pulled my own curtain. Once, when the curtain was about halfway up, the rope broke and the heavy roller dropped and hit me on the head. The performance was delayed fifteen minutes while I recovered from the shock. Many thought that was the best part of the show. The audience always enjoyed anything that went wrong during the show. At a time when women's skirts reached the floor, one of the show girls stood too close to the curtain roller. When it rolled up it caught the lower edge of her skirt and rolled it up also, exposing her stockinged calves and drawered legs (this at a time when the words "drawers" or "leg" were banned from refined conversation). The girl was so embarrassed and humiliated that she refused to work in the show that night.

Sometimes the stage consisted of a shaky platform at one end of the hall, with calico curtains across the corners to form dressing rooms. There might be a cloth front curtain, sliding on a crinkly wire which would not allow it to move easily.

At that time, there were no good lighting systems out in the country. At one place I used tallow candles with pie plates as reflectors for footlights. The hall proper was dimly lit by some poorly kept kerosene oil lights. The hall was so badly ventilated that when it was filled with oxygen consuming humans, there was not a sufficient amount of that gas to keep the lamps burning, and they would become dim. To remedy this situation, I had to stop the show and open the doors and windows so as to allow a supply of fresh air to enter. For seats, I used planks supported on nail kegs. The hall boasted a wheezy organ and a few other inconveniences like broken window panes, no lock on the door, and an inefficient janitor.

Generally the rent I paid for the hall always included janitor services. Most of the time a janitor's idea of taking care of a hall was to neglect it. He did about everything but attend to his duties, one of which was to start fires at 8 a.m. Seventy-five percent of the time I had to start them myself, or work in the cold. In order to be able to conduct my show alone, I had to work in the hall or theater all day. If the janitor was negligent in his janitorial duties, he was a past master in his ability to obtain free tickets to the show. His position as janitor entitled him to free tickets for himself and his family. The number of persons in the family was never mentioned. Those janitors had the largest families I ever heard of. If a poll were taken to determine who in the U.S. had the largest family, I am quite sure some small town hall janitor would win. His family started with his great grandfather, continuing to his great grandson, and they all expected free tickets to the show. Usually they got them. Most janitors were not endowed with an abundance of judgement, but they excelled in doing anything they should not do. They took a fiendish delight in emptying a bucket of coal into the stove at the time everyone was watching the levitation act in silence and amazement. Had the hypnotism and levitation been real, this imitation of a military barrage would have awakened the hypnotized subject and she would have fallen. Inasmuch as it was a stage act, nothing happened, unless it was that my blood pressure went up several notches (providing, of course, that people had blood pressure in those days).

While lampooning the janitors, who can no longer defend themselves, perhaps it would be no more than fair to tell about those who were unusual and unlike the ordinary run of broom pushers. An old gentleman who had charge of one hall had a personality different from the average small town citizen. Instead of the usual raiment of ragged overalls, he was dressed in a new, black suit of clothes. He wore a stiff bosom shirt and a black bow tie. He behaved himself in a most gentlemanly manner. I knew that he was a shoe repair man, but small town shoe repairers did not dress like senators or bankers. A few years earlier, he believed he was going to die. Being a methodical person, he decided to prepare for the important event. He purchased a cemetery lot and dug his grave. He made arrangements with the undertaker for burial. He purchased all his clothing and other necessities and calmly awaited the end, which failed to come. His health improved. He then met with some financial reverses which used up all of his available cash, and when he needed new clothing, he met the emergency by donning his burial attire.

The other janitor worthy of notice was a young man in his early twenties. He attended to the janitorial duties satisfactorily. When not employed he sat, untalkative, behind the hall stove and looked as though he felt sorry for himself. He dressed and acted like an ordinary farmer, but that was just what he was not. He was a remarkable arithmetician, what was called a lightning calculator. He could solve the most difficult problems in arithmetic, mentally. After glancing at as many as 50 numbers he would instantly give the sum. He could multiply numbers of four figures by other four figure numbers and never make an error. If he watched a person write 500 numbers on a sheet of paper he could repeat them all, in order, a year later. The principal of the school had taken him to a nearby city to give an exhibition of this work for some educators. They were so impressed that they secured some vaudeville engagements for him at a good salary. They fitted him with good street clothes and formal clothing for the stage. But when the time came for him to go to the city to fulfill his engagements, he refused to leave home. He said that God had given him those great talents, but not with which to earn money. If he used them to earn money he thought they would be taken from him. I never heard what became of him. He is probably still sweeping out dirty halls.

Probably the greatest punishment I had to endure while running a show was to be confined in a room with several hundred people for several hours. Not only was the air impure, but it also had an offensive odor, and odoriferous air was not conducive to my peace of mind. Besides bad breath, every person attending my show seemed to bring in an individual smell. As they stopped at the door to pay their admission, they would breathe on to my face and I had to inhale some of it. I exhaled it as fast as I could, of course, and probably some other person took it in. The odors were varied. One person would smell as though he had just finished eating an apple. Now a nice fresh apple does not smell so bad, but it is not so good second hand. A chewing gum breath could be tolerated. Grape smell was as bad as apples. The smell of soft drinks was intolerable. A tobacco breath did not help my disposition any. The eaters of strong smelling foods like sardines, old cheese, onions, and whiskey, did not smell like a nosegay.

The customers needing a bath had a stench of their own. On account of there being so many of them and because of their being so closely associated with each other, and with all of them needing a bath, they probably never even noticed the smell. One thing is certain, and that is that I did. In one place, people stood so close to me at the door that I had to put up a railing to keep them away from me. As there was no lumber yard where I could purchase a piece of timber, I went down the country road a short distance and helped myself to a rail from a farmer's fence to use as a dividing bar. This kept the people away from me, but not the odor. Most farmers brought in some nice, fresh barnyard soil on the bottoms of their shoes. Occasionally, there was a smell of a dead animal, like a rat or rabbit, from under the hall floor. When we played a fishing village, we had the additional advantage of the fish odor.

Probably the worst smelling hall I had was in a midwestern state. The hall was in a two-story building over what had once been a country store. I showed a week in that place. The odor was no worse than usual the first two days. Then, a stench began to fill the hall. It was worse than anything I had experienced. The lower story of the building was full of limburger cheese being stored there until it ripened. The process was slow, so a fire had been started in a stove to help it along. The warmth started the ripening, but it also ripened the odor which came up into my show hall full force. The natives did not seem to notice the odor at all. I was told that the heat was needed to cure the cheese. From the extra smell, I thought they had killed it and forgotten to embalm it. With the addition of the cheese odor to all those mentioned, the grand total was most delightful. I wished I could go back to the dry goods store where I had worked as a boy and enjoy the smell of calico and gingham. But at that, all of the hall odors combined were probably no worse than the city odors of garbage cans, lately occupied phone booths, unclean rest rooms, sewers, or crowded buses on rainy nights.

One might wonder how people could be expected to come to places like these. I also wondered, but they did come, and for over half a century I showed in such places for a week and nearly always had the hall filled every night. I gave an hour an a half show and changed my program each evening. Some individuals attended every night. My gross receipts were not large, as I charged a small admission, but my net profits were satisfactory. Expenses were low. I could rent a hall for as little as one dollar a night. No wonder there was a profit.

If the town happened to be incorporated, my next step was to see the mayor to obtain a permit or license to show. If the place was just one of those wide places in the road, this procedure was not necessary. Mayors were of two kinds, grouchy and mean, or pleasant and benevolent. If he happened to be the former, he might say, "Nope, we don't want no more shows here. They ain't good fer nothin' no how. They take all the money out of the town and don't do the town no good. Last show we had they all got drunk and raised hell all night in the tavern so nobody could sleep, and they had two young fellers who was meetin' two of our girls down by the railroad track after dark, and they wuzn't up to no good and if you come here to show you'll have to pay five dollars a day license." If the mayor were pleasant and benevolent, he would probably say, "Sure, come right along. We haven't had a show for a long time. This town needs something to liven it up a bit. Children always have a good time at a show. If you pay rent for a hall, we won't charge you a license."

People in small towns were always suspicious of strangers. It was probably because many strangers tried to and did defraud them in some way. When I first went into a little town I was always under suspicion. The town people would think I was using the show business as a subterfuge for some other activity. During the war, I was frequently thought to be a foreign spy. Just why a foreign spy might be spying in a little village of 100 people, located 1,000 miles from nowhere, never entered their minds. During prohibition, the natives thought I might be an Internal Revenue man on the lookout for dry law violators. Others thought I might be an escaped convict hiding from the authorities. I don't know what prompted them to think I might be a counterfeiter, unless it was because I had a collection of old coins. I joined a couple of lodges and that gave me a sort of a standing among my lodge brothers. Those lodge brothers had the utmost confidence in each other. They did not know that unscrupulous persons joined lodges for no other reason than to be able to cheat other lodge members.

The next problem was to find a hotel or place to board. Generally, there was no regular hotel and I had to look for a private home. Most families did not care to board show people. The general complaint against them was that they were either dirty, drunk, dopefiends, or that they did not pay their bills. From personal experience with many of them, I can certify this to have been the truth in many cases. After calling at many homes, I would finally find someone who would be willing to accommodate us. Accommodate was the word they used. I always thought it would be no accommodation, as I was going to pay for everything I received.

I was very particular in stating what my requirements were and in obtaining their promise that they would furnish them. Their promise did not mean a thing in many instances. During cold weather there was no heat in the room at one place. The old man I was renting from promised to put a stove in the room. When I arrived in town for the week's stay I found a stove but no stove pipe. I asked the old man if he were going to provide one. He said that he had only agreed to furnish a stove; he had not agreed to furnish a pipe. What's more, he did not furnish it. In order to have heat, I had to purchase fuel and a pipe. At one tumbled down shack there were no screens on the windows, and the mosquitos were plentiful. I asked my prospective landlord if he would put in some screen. He did not seem to comprehend what I meant. I told him to put something in the windows to keep out the insects. He said that he would. When I arrived to take possession of the room, I found that he had kept his promise. He had boarded them up with lumber. When I arrived in another town, I found the building where I was to stay burned to the ground. At still another time I found that the family which was to have boarded me had moved out of town and left me without a home.

I had several especially peculiar experiences. The oddest

one I ever had was with a couple of old maid sisters. I made arrangements in advance for a week's stay in their home. When we arrived in town to play the date, they refused to accept us and would give no reason why. Later we found out. They had consulted a Ouija Board and learned that we were scoundrels and deadbeats and would leave town without paying our debts. So they wanted no part of us. My greatest case of mistaken identity occurred in a little town on the Mississippi River. I was billed a week in advance, and during that week a very old woman walked the streets and called at homes to plead with people not to have anything to do with me. She said that I would break up families and would take many of the home folks along with me when I left. No one could understand what she meant. When I arrived in town to show, we solved the mystery. On one of my bills I had the word "Spiritualism," and the woman had it confused with Mormonism. Many years before, when she was a little girl, the Mormons had made a stop in the town on their trek west, preached, made converts, and taken some local people along with them. The poor soul thought this performance was due for a repetition.

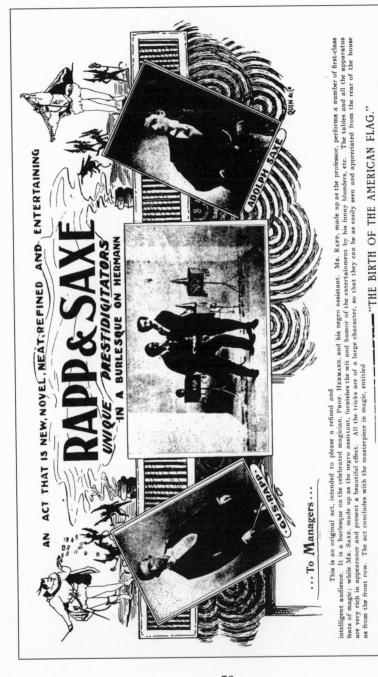

AN ACT THAT IS NEW, NOVEL, NEAT, REFINED AND ENTERTAINING

RAPP & SAXE

UNIQUE PRESTIDIGITATORS
IN A BURLESQUE ON HERMANN

ADOLPH SAXE

GUS RAPP

...To Managers...

This is an original act, intended to please a refined and intelligent audience. It is a burlesque on the celebrated magician, PROF. HERMANN, and his negro assistant. MR. RAPP, made up as the professor, performs a number of first-class feats of magic; while MR. SAXE, made up as the negro assistant, furnishes the wit and humor of the entertainment by his funny blunders, etc. The tables and all the apparatus are very rich in appearance and present a beautiful effect. All the tricks are of a large character, so that they can be as easily seen and appreciated from the rear of the house as from the front row. The act concludes with the masterpiece in magic, entitled ————"THE BIRTH OF THE AMERICAN FLAG."

This consists in the production from a borrowed hat, of flags of all nations, which are thrown in the air when they change to a large American flag, size 9x15 ft. This is a startling finale and arouses the enthusiasm of the audience. Special music has been arranged to suit the act. This act can be produced only on a first-class stage, therefore we can play nothing but first-class houses. We can furnish half-tone engravings for advertising purposes. If you want a novelty, book us.

76

CHAPTER FIVE

HOTELS DE LUXE

There were three kinds of small town country hotels —
bad, worse, and worst. All of them were the bane of the old time
showman's life. The dictionary defines the word "bane" as
being anything pernicious or noxious. I am not quite sure what
these two words mean, but they sound repulsive enough to
describe the 1880-90 country hotels. If there happened to be
a rickety building in a small town that was not suitable for
anything at all, some irresponsible persons would automatically gravitate to it and decide to open a hotel. The fact that
they might not be mentally competent or did not have funds to
finance such a project was a matter of little importance.

The personnel of a hotel usually consisted of a family
without any visible means of support. Nearly always there
would be a man, his wife and daughter, and sometimes a son
who appeared to be there for no good reason at all. The typical
landlord was frequently a fat middle-aged man who gave the
impression that he was dirty and lazy. His ambition was to be
in a business where his wife could do most of the work, and the
hotel business was it. The landlady, who was also the cook,
wore dirty clothes, emphasized by a greasy apron. If there was
a waitress, she was nearly always the daughter of the dirty
cook. They were not an appetizing trio. Maybe quartet if we
include the half-witted son.

All hotel dining rooms had one fault in common and that
was that they were cold during the winter season and hot and
without window screens during summer, when insects were
numerous. Of course, there would be a fire in the stove during

77

cold weather, but this fire would be started only a few minutes before the large brass bell announcing that the meal was ready was sounded. It would be burned out before the meal was over. Food would be brought in hot from the kitchen only to become cold before it could be eaten.

The food was always of a poor quality and not properly cooked, and if one happened to be unfortunate enough to get a glimpse of the kitchen one's appetite was most definitely not improved. The cheap silverware used at these hotels was not worth stealing. There were no napkins. If one happened to get food on his fingers, he just licked it off or wiped it on his clothing. Of course a few carried handkerchiefs; the large, red bandanna kind. One man wiped his greasy fingers on his beard. I would not be surprised that if he washed his beard he would reclaim enough grease, leftover food morsels, etc., to make a bowl of soup.

If any of these substandard imitations of hotels ever served any palatable food, they were few and far between and I was not able to discover many of them. One time we had half fried pancakes. I called to the old lady cook out in the kitchen, "Mother, these cakes are not done." She answered, "They be so done." "No," I said, "they are still raw in the middle." "Well, for land sakes," she called back. "Can't you eat around the edges?" The food was always served in what seemed to be unclean dishes, probably to match the hands of the dirty waitress. Once when the cook, who was also the waitress, was unusually dirty, I remarked about it to one of the other boarders (who was not far removed from the superlative of dirt). He laughed and said, "Yep, she is purty dirty. We wuz goin't to take up a collection to git money to send her to a laundry to git the dirt scoured offen her, but we wuz afraid we wouldn't git nothin' back and we wouldn't have no cook."

While the food was poor in quality, there was always a generous quantity. I never cared to eat the hash they served unless I was personally acquainted with the cook, and in some instances, not then. Most hash tasted as though it might be the reincarnation of every animal that had died recently. And the butter was always rancid. Oleo margarine and ice boxes were not known out in the country at the early period I am writing about. At one place, we were served something that looked and smelled like inferior meat. We did not eat it. It was back on the table at the next meal. Again we did not eat it. When it was served for the third time, my wife wrapped it up in her handkerchief and disposed of it. Something called pie was served. If there were more than one kind, it made little difference which was selected, because they all tasted the same; that is, bad. It is said that a man is what he eats. If that is true, after eating at country hotels for more than half a century, I must resemble a garbage can full of a heterogeneous conglomeration of half decayed vegetable and animal matter. No wonder I never got fat. Experienced eaters at country hotels never found fault with the food. They just ate it and allowed the different kinds to fight it out among themselves on the inside. No one ever heard of a glutton, and nothing was said about dieting in those days.

Those persons (hotel patrons were never called guests) who did not pay the transient rate were termed boarders. They paid a low weekly rate. Those who did pay the higher, transient rate were called travelling men. The former ate at a long table where the food was served in large dishes and each person helped himself. The travelling men ate at small tables. The food served at both tables was the same, with the exception that there was a bowl of wrinkled apples on the transient table. This reminds me of an incident which occurred out west. The hotel owner was an odd character who spoke with a German accent. A local person could eat at the long table and be charged twenty cents for his meal. The transients or visitors had to pay fifty cents for a meal at the table with the apples on it. The guests would pay for their meals at the desk as they left the dining room.

The conversation during such a payment ran somewhat like this. Guest: "How much for my meal, landlord?" Landlord: "Did you ead at de dable mid de epples on?" Guest: "No, I ate at the long table." Landlord: "Den dot will be dwendy-five cends." Next Guest: "How much?" Landlord: "Did you ead at de dable mid de epples on?" Guest: "Yes, I did." Landlord: "Den dot will be fifty cends." After listening to this line of conversation repeated several times, one bright transient tried to fool the land lord. When he was asked, "Did you ead at de dable mid de epples on?" he answered, "No, I ate at the long table." The landlord looked surprised, but was equal to the occasion. He quickly said, "Dot will be fifty cends, because you should have ead at de dable mid de epples on." Having no money for furnishings, the landlords would equip their hotels with homemade fittings or furniture from the second-hand store. The office would have a rough lumber desk, sometimes unpainted. There would be a few round back chairs, and rooms would be illuminated by smoky coal oil lamps which always needed trimming or were out of oil. A wooden water bucket equipped with a long handled tin dipper served for drinking.

Most of the bedrooms had no real comforts of any kind. They had no carpets or rugs. Some of them had a chair and a stand with a wash bowl and pitcher that had survived the Civil War. The towel was many times made from old flour or sugar sack. It was changed only on urgent demand. The occupants of those rooms not favored with a wash bowl pitched and laved themselves in the hall, using a tin wash basin and yellow scrubbing soap. Of course, everyone used the same towel. A bed being an absolute necessity, there was always one in the room. But what a bed. There was hardly ever a bedspring, and the mattress resting on wooden slats was packed solid by long usage.

Sometimes there were no sheets, and when they were changed, which was less often than the towels, they were not always clean. If not too dirty, the sheets would be ironed without washing .When we saw the ironed creases by the aid of a dim coal oil lamp we would accept them as being clean. During the winter season, the rooms were so cold that the water in the pitcher was frozen by morning. When the landlord called us for breakfast he would leave a container of hot water on the floor outside of the door. This was all right, if one could get out of the bed and to the door before that water also became cold. Half of the time there was no key to lock the door, and on one occasion there was no door.

I always investigated the hotels to find out if they were clean or not. There was no positive way this could be done. A look into the office and dining room might show these two rooms to be all right, while the kitchen, which could not be inspected, might be filthy. I did, however, have a method to judge the condition of the kitchen without seeing it. I would take a look into that little structure, located in the rear of every well appointed hotel, and which for want of a better name was vulgarly named a backhouse. If the seat of that usually dirty edifice was clean, I was reasonably certain that the kitchen was also clean. There were no health laws at that time, cleanliness was not next to godliness, and neither was it a hotel commodity. Sometimes it was not at all. I would always ask to see the rooms, so that I could examine the bed. The simple minded country folk could not understand why each new guest should have clean bed linen. When examining one bed, I saw that the sheets had not been changed after the last sleeper because there were yellow and bloody stains on the sheets near the foot of the bed. When I called the attention of the landlady to this fact, she said, "Why that's nothin' to worry about. My son had a running sore on his ankle and he slept there last night, but it ain't nothin' ketchin' and he ain't dirty." However, I did worry about it, and I worried her until she changed the sheets.

Besides being very smelly and unclean, the beds were sometimes occupied by a class of free boarders known as bedbugs. I am quite sure that when Noah took a pair of all animals into the ark, he was careless in selecting his bedbugs. I think he took a pair of healthy females loaded with fertilized eggs. I always had to take precautionary measures to prevent us from getting into bed buggy hotels. The only way to find out about this was to ask the hotel keeper point blank if he did or did not have them. This question was an offensive one and usually produced of an offensive answer. If he had no bugs he would not be offended, but if he did have them he (or she) was ready with a militant answer.

One woman retorted by saying, "Young man (I was young then), I'd have you understand there is not a single bedbug in my house." I felt like answering her with the old-time blackface monologist joke of that time, that if there were not any single ones, they were probably all married and had large families. Believing her assurances that there were no such "varmits" in her bed, I arranged for room and board for a week. The first night, the bugs were so thick we had to sit up all night. This did not keep them from crawling up the chair legs to reach us and try to satisfy their appetite. To prevent this, we spread vaseline on squares of paper and put one under each chair leg. The pesky little critters would not crawl on the vaseline. A few of them reached us via another route. They crawled up the walls and out on the ceiling above us and dropped down on us. However, we saw them coming and brushed them away. My wife impaled a large number of them on a needle, which she presented to the landlady in the morning. The woman gave one shriek and said, "Good heavens, I didn't know that there were bugs in that bed, and I put our minister there to sleep night before last! How will I ever be able to face him again?" We did not know and we were not interested in solving that problem for her as we were too busy looking for another place to board.

A bewhiskered, grizzly bear specimen of humanity once answered, "Yep, we got plenty of bedbugs and they're bigger and hungrier than any you ever met in the West or South and if you ain't man enough to fight a few harmless bugs you won't stand no show with the rough men and boys around here who will try to break up your show, and you better git out o' town quick." Which I did.

One hotel keeper gave me the surprise of my young life when he said, "You needn't be afraid of bugs; we got 'em, all right, but we keep 'em all in one bed." This was a new one on me, and I asked, "Just how do you manage to do that?" "Well," he explained, "they stay in that one room because that is the only place where they can get a jag on." Holy mackerel, intoxicated bedbugs! Who ever heard of anything like that? Further questioning brought out the information that a man who slept in that bed was a confirmed drunkard. He would come home every night saturated with alcohol, and as soon as he was asleep the bugs would suck his blood and become apparently lifeless. He said he collected a number of the bugs at different times and put them, inactive, into a small box. The next morning they would be lively as ever. He promised to give a demonstration when we came to stop at his hotel. This never took place because we never stopped at this hotel. We even skipped the town. About the only favorable comment I can make about the country hotels of those days is that there were no highjacking bellhops looking for tips; but if the hotels were putrid, so were many of the members of small shows. For this reason, many of the hotels did not care to "take in" show people. The grievances against them were that in most cases they were dirty, ill-mannered. Some of them did not pay their bills, some couples were not married, or perhaps one of the male members tried to induce the wife of a local man to elope with him. I know of one case when this did happen. One complaint was against a married couple with a baby who used the pillow cases for diapers and left them behind for the hotel people to wash. The manager of a small dramatic show, unable to pay its hotel bill, left a diamond ring as a guarantee of payment promising to redeem it in a few weeks. The promise was never kept, and when the diamond was inspected, it was found to be an artificial stone of little value. The manager of this show told me that he carried a quantity of these rings for use in paying his bills whenever he could negotiate the project. One woman did not like show people because they would not arise in the morning for five o'clock breakfast. I never could imagine why small town people arose so early. After having lived among them for so many years, I can only conclude that they were fearful that if they slept late, they would miss something said or done.

A hawk-faced female whom I was trying to inveigle into boarding us said, "No, I reckon I won't keep no more show people. The last show we had here had a woman with them who wasn't respectable." I asked, "What made you think that?" She looked around furtively to make sure no one was listening and almost whispered, "She smoked cigarettes; she must have been a bad woman." "Did you actually see her smoke?" I asked. "No," she answered, "but after she was gone I cleaned her room and the floor was full of cigarette bottoms (meaning butts), and I don't want no more such trash in my house." I agreed with her that the woman must have been a very bad one, and I also convinced her that we were respectable people who did not smoke cigarettes, so she accepted us. I took so much time trying to convince the local people that we were respectable that I finally believed it to be a fact.

I never would pay my hotel expenses in advance, as was sometimes demanded, because as soon as they had our money, all interest in our welfare was gone. Meals would be more inferior than ever, not ready on time, or perhaps not ready at all. Room work would be neglected. One landlord and his wife actually left town for a visit without notifying us, and we had to forage for ourselves for a few days.

The dirtiest place we had was when we boarded with an old man and woman who were so filthy that we could not eat their food. We asked them to furnish us with unshelled, hard boiled eggs. These we knew were clean. We bought boxed crackers, which were also clean, and took these to the hotel with us. For a whole week we subsisted on crackers and eggs.

One very peculiar happening which did not affect us much occurred to a very nice man and wife with whom we were sojourning. They had a good reputation in the town, belonged to a church, and were interested in public affairs. The wife had a man friend with whom she had been acquainted since childhood. He was coming to visit them for a few days, and while the couple never made a habit of drinking anything intoxicating, they thought they would lay in a supply of wet goods to entertain the guest. While we were at the hall in the evening, giving the show, they all became tipsy and their speech somewhat incoherent. The wife said that the house had a slight mortgage on it and that she had some money in the bank to use to pay the indebtedness.

The husband became provoked and said that it was his duty to pay such debts, and that she should save her money. The visitor broke in by saying that if she was damn fool enough to pay the debt, he should allow her to do it. The husband, who did not like to have his wife called a damn fool, became infuriated and hauled off and slugged the visitor under the jaw. He fell to the floor unconscious. The wife became hysterical and grabbed the phone to call the doctor. The husband took the phone from her and hit her in the face with it, blackening her eye and cutting a gash in her cheek. She also fell to the floor unconscious. The husband became panic stricken. Thinking he had killed them, he placed the muzzle of a deer rifle at his heart and pulled the trigger. He fell to the floor, unconscious. A neighbor who heard the shot investigated and called the state police. By the time they arrived, the three warriors had returned to consciousness. The police took the husband to the hospital and the wife and visitor to jail. The next morning the fact was disclosed that no one was seriously injured. The bullet from the rifle had missed the husband's heart, and he was released from the hospital in three days. The wife and visitor could go home at once. As no one would testify against another, the police could not bring a charge against them. While they were all away from home we had to do our own cooking and chamber work. The visitor did not return. The man and wife were so humiliated by the affair that they sold their home and moved to another town. Moral: Don't visit with childhood acquaintances, especially if they like whiskey.

Another unpleasant incident concerns a Christmas dinner. The family we were staying with received an invitation to come to a neighbor's home for an evening Christmas dinner. My wife and I were included in the invitation. Since they did not plan having to do much cooking that day, the folks I boarded with did not lay in any food supply. Toward evening, as we were about to leave to go to the neighbor's home, we received a message telling us not to come. We found out why the next day. They had purchased a large turkey and everything necessary for an elaborate dinner, and the wife had the meal cooked when an unexpected visitor arrived. It was the wife's sister, who came a long way from a distant state. The sister was welcome even though she was intoxicated. Not only was she filled up inside, but she also brought a bountiful supply of whiskey in bottles on the outside. To keep her sister company, the wife also tanked up. The food was cooking, but with the cook intoxicated it was not attended to, and the turkey and everything else was so badly burned that it could not be eaten. When we could not go to the neighbors for dinner, something had to be prepared at home. This was not an easy thing to do with no food supply on hand and the nearby store was closed for the Christmas holiday. All that could be found to make a meal was potatoes, bread, butter, and coffee, and that was just what we had for Christmas dinner. We were glad to have even that little, because we were hungry.

While on the subject of Christmas dinners, I might just as well tell of another experience on that day. This time there was just an old lady with a daughter who was not very bright. There was an unusually disagreeable odor about the house, which we thought was coming from the woman's clothing when she stood with her back near a hot stove. We discovered that it came from a barrel of sauerkraut which she kept in a clothes closet off of the living room. When meals were over, the daughter would go around the tables and drink the small amount of coffee that was left in the cups. She would swirl the cups around so as to be sure to get the sugar left in them. The old woman was, or pretended to be, very religious. Every night after going to bed we would hear her praying to the Lord to forgive her sins and to forgive the sins of the world at large. Also, she would pray for the strangers under her roof (meaning us), that they might see the errors of their ways and reform. Her sin consisted of giving us food that was unfit to eat. I was told that when she attended church suppers she wore a double skirt, like those used by shop lifters, into which she would slyly slip all the food she could steal. I believe this, because for Christmas dinner we had frankfurters, which was what they had served at the church supper two nights before.

When there was no such animal as a hotel, we had to find refuge with some family. Sometimes these places were very good and we would spend an enjoyable week, but when they were bad they were very bad. Usually only poor families would bother to board people, and being poor, they furnished poor accommodations. They probably did the best they could for us. When they promised to treat us as though we belonged to the family, we usually looked for another place. We also looked for another place when they kept a pet pig in the house, which is what one family did. But good or bad, we always became intimately acquainted with the people we boarded with. We would have to look at the tintype photos of relatives in the plush covered family album. This was a lesson in ancient history. We had to play with children who needed a nose wipe. When we had to hold the baby, there was always the problem of clothing renovation. The last private home we stopped at was the filthiest of all. When some coffee was spilled on the oilcloth table covering, the waitress used a still damp and dirty baby's diaper to wipe it off. This caused me to do something which brought about a drastic change in my mode of living. From then on, we had no more dirty landlords, bad meals, uncomfortable beds, cold rooms, and bedbugs, because I purchased a house trailer.

I have good reason to believe that I lived in the very first house trailer. I had one before automobiles were known. It was a homemade house on wheels, trailed behind another house on wheels, which was drawn by horses. On one occasion, it was drawn by a traction engine which was a self-propelled vehicle, a sort of crude automobile. That house trailer was a delightful piece of property. It was a home away from home, and had all the inconveniences of an inconvenient home. When one looked at the empty trailer, there seemed to be plenty of room. As soon as one took in a fishpole and a small can of sardines, the place would be crowded. The ordinary sized trailer accommodated four persons if they stood. If they tried to sit, the place would be crowded. There would be plenty of room for one person, but even he would have to go outside to turn around or to change a ten dollar bill. A man, wife, two children and a dog might manage to get along, if the children and the dog slept under the trailer. The big advantage of the trailer was that one could stop anywhere and be at home. When trailers were new and a novelty, one could stop anywhere and be welcome. Some people would allow parking on their front lawn.

During the winter the trailer could be kept cosy and warm with a kerosene heater, but the windows and doors would have to be closed and then there would be no ventilation. The heater would soon use all the oxygen, and along with cooking and other smells, the place would soon have an odor like an ancient kitchen. There was one cold night when my wife awakened me to tell me that she smelled a disagreeable odor. She believed it to come from my socks and insisted that I should put them out-of-doors. I arose and evicted the offending tenants. I went back to sleep and was awakened again and told that the odor still persisted, and that it must come from my shoes. So I arose and ousted the shoes. The odor continued, and I refused to pay further attention to it. My wife arose and went on an exploring expedition. She soon discovered the offensive culprit. It was an uncovered dish of sauerkraut which she had forgotten to put in the ice box. Early in the morning it rained and when I awoke I found my hose and shoes nearly ruined.

Not all experiences with the trailer were satisfactory. There was the time when I forgot to attach the trailer to the auto and drove fifteen miles before I discovered that I was without a home. I had to retrace my route to hunt for it. I found it at the starting point. Another time it became unhooked while on the road. I went back to hunt for it and found it in a field of potatoes along side of the road. I had to hire a team of horses to pull it back on the highway. Once it had a flat tire, which I did not discover until the tire and rim were ruined. Always, I had to remember that a license fee was due at the beginning of the year. Later, I acquired an up-to-date trailer with all modern equipment. An owner of one of these high priced trailers never went outside to change a ten dollar bill because he never had one until the trailer was paid for. All the inconveniences of the primitive trailer were gone, except the license fee.

RAPP'S
NOVELTY
AND
COMEDY CO.

PRESENTING

A Refined and Moral Entertainment

The Floating Fairy

The Body of a Living Woman Suspended in Mid-Air without Any Support. A Most Beautiful Illusion

The Stovepipe Mystery

A European Novelty—Puzzling in the Extreme

Serpentine - Butterfly - Rainbow Dances

ILLUSTRATED SONGS

A Novelty Musical Act !

Introducing Solos on Cowbells, Bottles, Tin Whistles, Horse Shoes, China Bowls and Tin Cans, and Also Musical Glasses
PRODUCING THE SWEETEST MUSIC ON EARTH

The Spiritualistic Seance

Spiritualism Viewed from a Religious and Scientific Standpoint
Slatewriting—Materialization—Trumpet Messages—
Psychical Manifestations

SUBSTITUTION

A Bewildering Illusion !   Come and See It !

Imperial Marionettes

A Complete Entertainment in Themselves !
SEE THE DANCING SKELETON !

COMEDY SKETCHES
You Smile
You Laugh
You Roar

Gazette Show Print, Mattoon, Ill.

CHAPTER SIX

THE SHOW

A day's work for me was a day and night's work of about fifteen hours. I had to arise at 7:30 a.m., and from that time until 10:30 p.m. I was busy. Perhaps there had been a storm during the night and I had lost three hours' sleep. I had to arise at 7:30 just the same. After breakfast, I made the rounds of the tent to tighten the ropes, which had been purposely loosened by tipping the poles the night before. If the ropes had not been loosened, the moisture in the night air would cause them to shrink and tear the tent. This took half an hour of my time. Next, I unpacked and arranged all of the things needed for that night's show. As I gave quite an elaborate performance, this took quite some time.

While I was engaged with this work, a boy might come from the phone office telling me that someone had phoned from Punktown and that if I wanted to play that town next week, I would have to come over and contract for the hall at once, as other parties wanted it. This meant that I had to rush to the livery stable, hire a horse and buggy, and start out on a ten mile drive. I arrived in Punktown too late for the hotel dinner and had to go to the grocery store and buy some crackers and bananas. After contracting for the hall, hunting a place to board, and billing the town, I had to drive ten miles back home. This made a twenty mile drive in an uncomfortable buggy, with slow horses, over rough roads.

By the time I arrived home, I had a backache and it was near evening. My wife then told me that there was a hole in the tent which needed patching. So, I had to tackle that job.

Then, along came the bill boys, and I had to date a lot of bills with a rubberstamp. About this time, I remembered that my light plant had not operated just right last night, and I would have to see what I could do for that. The governor belt was worn and loose, so I made another one out of an old trousers belt. It was a good thing that I was a jack of all trades and could help myself. By this time it was 6 p.m. and I was tired and dirty, hungry and ill-tempered. Who wouldn't be? My hands were greasy and black from the work I had done on the light plant. It took quite a lot of scrubbing to get them clean enough so I could exhibit them as the most skillful hands in the world. I hardly ever had time enough for a leisurely evening meal. I was always in a hurry because I was always behind with my work. As soon as the meal was over, I had to go to the show tent and make more preparations for the evening. The entrance had to be opened. The seats had to be inspected to see if they were properly adjusted so that they would not tip over, injure someone, and cause a damage suit to be put against me. I heard people congregating on the outside and clamoring for admission. It was opening time, but I had to give the stage another quick inspection to see if everything was properly arranged. Some more clamoring, but I was still not ready for them to enter. I tried to close the front curtain to find that the pull ropes had to be untangled. More clamoring at the entrance, and I was becoming nervous. I started the lighting plant and discovered that two light bulbs had burned out and had to be replaced. More clamoring. Then I had to count out change for my money box and put paper money in my pocket so as to be able to change large bills.

Finally I arrived at the door, fifteen minutes late and was ready for the patrons to enter. I always stood at the door and collected from the fold as they entered. When I had to leave to start the show, I would delegate this activity to any local person. I had no way of determining if he turned in the right amount of money. In the many years that I did this, however, I never had reason to think that anyone cheated me out of a cent. About this time, most of them would change their minds and decide that they did not want to enter for a while. If a few of them did come in, they wanted to go out again. There was always something to vex me at the door. A man would not want to pay for a boy who was almost old enough to vote. One little boy presented a ticket which was legal tender at his last school play and left crying when I wouldn't accept it for admission. When the tent was full and I was just going to start the show, the lights dimmed and went out. Hastily, I gave the money box to the nearest person and asked him to collect while I corrected the trouble. There was no trouble. In my hurry, I had forgotten to put gasoline in the engine tank, so the engine stopped and the lights stopped too. I got it going again and put on my stage clothes, and I was ready to start.

Away back in the good old days most of the country people came to the villages by way of horse and buggy, though some came by other means. Those having a short distance to go would walk in. Some of the boys would come on horseback. As they neared the village, they would shoot revolvers, probably in imitation of the bad boys of the West. Jesse James was a hero among the younger generation at that time. It was nothing unusual to see a man, his wife, and a child riding one horse. Sometimes a man would walk in with a child on his shoulders. A hayrack filled with straw, men, women, and children was a common sight during the winter season. One man loaded three children into a wheelbarrow and pushed them in. Another man had to cross a bridge-less creek, swollen by continued rains. His method of crossing was a very easy one. Without removing his clothing, he swam the creek. He was soaking wet during the show, but he seemed to enjoy it the same as anyone else. During a conversation with one of my patrons, he told me that the flooded river completely surrounded his house. When asked how he managed to get to dry land, he said that the water was only about a foot deep and he only had to wade half a mile. However, he left his wife and children at home on the temporary island.

People of the small towns did love to get the best of the showman by getting into the show without paying the admission price. Various and clever were the schemes they tried; some of them were legitimate, while others were not. Occasionally they deceived me, but most of the time they did not. In the opinion of the country folk of that day, the showman was a very superior being, and they felt a lot of satisfaction at being able to fool him.

Here is how some little girls managed to obtain some free tickets. One spring afternoon, we were in an upstairs hall; from the windows we could overlook the whole village. A little girl brought us a bouquet of home garden flowers. This friendly act so pleased my wife that she gave the little stranger a hearty thank you and a complimentary ticket to the show. The girl left in a hurry and scampered down the street. In a short time another little miss came with flowers. She also received a free ticket. Soon, two more girls with flowers appeared, and two more tickets were dispensed. Fifteen minutes later, I looked out of the window and it appeared as though there was a little girl emerging from every yard in the village. They all received free tickets, and we had enough common or garden variety flowers to start a second class florist shop. The old fashioned square piano was covered with them. At the show that night I made an announcement to the effect that while we appreciated flowers, we could not accept any more. This was a clever and harmless trick on the part of the little girls, and it amused us greatly.

There were other instances, however, in which the methods were not quite so innocent. One town had some boys who found out that by using mercury and vinegar, they could plate a one-cent coin so that it somewhat resembled a dime. I accepted a few of these before I discovered the deception. Some boys resorted to counterfeiting. The soil in their locality was heavy red clay. They used this for making molds of five-cent pieces and half dollars. Into these they poured molten lead, the result being a metal coin or a reasonable facsimile thereof. As this law violation occurred in a section where there was little or no law enforcement, the boys were able to get away with it. A few of these sham coins were passed on to me. On leaving the theatre one Halloween night, I found the windows of the ticket office smeared with white soap. The next morning two small boys came to the theatre and offered to clean the windows if I would give them passes for the show. This I did with pleasure. Soon afterwards, someone informed me that those were the boys who had put the soap on the windows. A group of small boys in one place who were minus admission money congregated in the hall and laughed and talked and stamped their feet to make enough noise to disturb the show. The hall manager would go out and chase them away, but they would return and continue the noise. The only way to quiet them was to allow them to go into see the show free, which was done.

One night a woman came to the door carrying a six year old boy. She asked, "Have I gotta pay for a baby?" "What baby?" I asked. "This one here," she said, indicating the boy in her arms. "But," I said, "that big boy isn't a baby." "Why not," she replied, "a child is a baby as long as it nurses, isn't it?" "Sure," I said, "but that big boy doesn't nurse." "Doesn't he? Let me show you," she said. "Come Cedric, get your supper." Then followed an open and above board demonstration that the big boy did nurse. I hastily gave Cedric a free admission ticket. One man came in carrying a big boy and asked, "Do I have to pay for this little boy?" I answered, "That boy is above the age limit and you will have to pay for him." Angrily, he dropped the boy to his feet, growling, "Well, if I gotta pay for you, then you walk." Early birds coming to the show would clamor to be admitted to the theatre. This meant they would have to wait an hour until the show started. Consequently, they would have to find some way of amusing themselves during that hour. Older people would visit with their friends. Everybody was acquainted with everyone else. Farmers might talk over matters pertaining to their activities. Perhaps some hired help might be secured. A calf might be sold, or they might even make a horse trade. Being able to meet friends and attend to such matters was what helped to attract farmers to the show. Another reason for their coming to the show was that ancient excuse for going to the circus, and that was that they had to take the children. The get-together before my show was a sort of community meeting. If they went to the larger places nearby, they might have cushioned chairs, brilliant lighting and other embellishments; but they would be seated among strangers, they would feel uncomfortable, and above all, they could not expectorate tobacco juice on the floor.

The young folk and the older ones with nothing special to interest them had to devise other ways of passing the time. This they did by running, yelling, screaming, fighting, and raising a rumpus in general until pandemonium reigned supreme. Throwing peanuts at each other was considered the ultimate in sport. Hitting the face of an unsuspecting person with a peanut and seeing him jump provoked many screams and much laughter. Blowing up empty peanut sacks and popping them added to the din. When a show came to town the general store stocked up on peanuts, knowing there would be a big demand for them. Those who could not afford to throw away peanuts brought an ear of corn and used corn kernels instead of peanuts. All this was a lot of harmless fun until a corn kernel hit a little girl's eye and she nearly lost her vision. This spelled finis for the sport at my show. If I had all the peanuts and corn kernels swept out of the halls during my sixty years of showing, I could realize a substantial sum on their sale.

There were always some broken chairs in the country "oprey." The janitor would place these in another room so they would not be used. Small boys (sometimes big ones) would slyly secure several of these and place them among the perfect ones. Then, they would watch for someone to sit on one and laugh and scream and clap their hands when the chair collapsed and the person fell to the floor. If he had broken his neck, the amusement would have been just as great. Another favorite diversion was to pull the chair from under a person just as he was about to sit on it. The ancient pastime of putting a tack or bent pin on a chair was not neglected. They also delighted in putting a chocolate drop on a chair, with the fond hope that some woman with white garments would sit on it. The king of all small town amusement devices was a long wooden bench with a longitudinal crack from end to end in the seat plank. Normally the crack was slightly open, but when someone sat on the board it bent just enough to close the crack and pinch the skin of the sitter, causing him (or her) to jump. To the people of the small town, nothing in the world could be funnier, especially if the victim happened to be a woman of generous proportions.

Sometimes I had to leave my station at the door and go to the front of the stage to make a request for better order. This would quiet them but not for long. With adults talking, babies crying, and small children running, yelling and screaming, disorder was a mild name for it. No matter how much noise and confusion existed, the persons in my audience were usually quiet and attentive once the show started.

Once in a while, however, some peculiar persons were among them. One woman came to the show and sat with her back to the stage the whole evening. This was something unusual, and it nearly gave me stage fright. I had to ask to find out the reason. The woman was a visitor from another town who did not "believe in shows." The family she was visiting lived in a house where a murder had been committed. The house was said to be haunted. The whole family insisted on going to my show, which would have left the visitor alone in the house; and as she was afraid to stay there, she had to go along to the show. But rather than have the sin of having witnessed a stage show on her soul, she sat with her back to the stage and cotton stuffed in her ears. Another peculiar incident was that of a woman who came to the show in ragged clothing, her face masked with a cheap masquerade false face. She was an Indian who lived on a nearby reservation. She had been convicted of some law violation, but had been paroled with the stipulation that she must not leave the reservation, the limit of which was only a half-mile from where I was showing. She wanted to attend the show but was fearful that someone might see her and report her to the authorities. So, she adopted the disguise and sneaked into the rear of the theater after the show started and left just before it was over. Then she hurried to the reservation.

There was one young man with a raucous laugh resembling a braying mule. He was not able to control this and when he brayed at a show, his laugh threw the performers into a state of confusion. This amused the audience very much, and someone always paid his admission to a show just to have him furnish the fun. Fortunately, someone told me about him in advance and, being prepared, I was not bothered by him at all. A woman with a large metal ear trumpet aimed at me was a nerve wrecker. But the worst audience nuisance was the crying baby. Mothers would allow them to cry all through the show without making an effort to remove them. Sometimes I felt like committing infanticide. On my advertising I sometimes included this line: "Good Babies Admitted Free. If they cry, it's $10."

A noisy crowd meant good door receipts and was preferable to the quietness of a small attendance. Small crowds were the exception rather than the rule, but they were a pain in the neck. I always opened the door for admissions at seven o'clock. If I was having good attendance, some persons would be ready to enter. If it was a poor town, there might be a long wait before the first customers came. One very cold night I was ready as usual. The heating stove was near the entrance, and we were huddled about it looking for some signs of life. Footsteps at the outer door told us that people were approaching. They were three bill boys who had billed the village for free tickets to the show. Another wait, and some more footsteps. This time it was the house manager and his family, who were also admitted free. Next came the janitor's family, also free customers. It was nearly starting time when I remarked to the janitor that it looked as though there would not be enough people to show to. "Oh yes there will be," he said. "In just a few minutes there will be a good crowd here. A lot of people are just leaving their homes now."

Sure enough, in a short time the hall was nearly filled. I could hardly wait until the show was over to ask the janitor how he could tell when people were leaving their homes, while he was inside of a building on a night so dark that he could not have seen farther than ten feet had he been outside. The solution to this mystery was a simple one. Everyone in town used gas for heating. When people left their homes, they turned down their gas flame as a matter of safety. Turning down the gas in about fifty homes increased the pressure in the hall stove. This made the flame in the hall stove roar. The janitor could hear this, and that was how he knew. Not all janitors were dumb, just most of them.

Sometimes I had peculiar experiences with off-stage shows. While driving across country in the South, I came upon a prison chain gang. Because of the rough condition of the road I had to stop for a while. Knowing from the appearance of the outfit that I had a show, the overseer asked me to give an exhibition during the noon hour. This I did. About thirty rough-looking customers with leg irons appreciated the half hour show I gave them. They sat on a schoolhouse lawn, and I used the building and some bushes for a background. They had a kitchen truck, and a guard asked me if I would like some sandwiches. Being hungry, I accepted. In a short time I was presented with twenty–four ham sandwiches, enough of such food to last the rest of my life. At another time I gave a private performance for four Catholic nuns. This was an odd but appreciative quartet. But giving a private show for an eighty year old lady and a four year old boy was not anything to become overly enthusiastic about. Neither was giving a show for a boy in bed with a broken leg. Probably the most peculiar magic show I ever gave was one for three monkeys. A professor of some kind of "ology" was studying evolution and was experimenting with monkeys. He wanted to note how they would react to color changing handkerchiefs and similar tricks. I did my best to entertain the little brutes, but if they did any reacting, I did not notice it. I did notice that I did not get any applause, and neither did I get a return engagement.

No matter where they were, my audience paid close attention or they would miss some of the tricks. In the old days, there was always a rough class of men and boys in the larger places who delighted in causing disturbances at political meetings, church services, shows, or public gatherings of any kind. My show was remarkably free from such disorders. In the smaller places, there were a few who would have enjoyed annoying me, but they were a minority group. The majority of the people in every community were my friends and would have violently opposed any of the trouble makers, had they tried to interfere with my show. There were a few incidents, though, about trouble, which was not trouble, which are worth relating.

Someone was collecting admission money for me while I was giving the show. An intoxicated Indian was refused admission. He cursed so long and so loud outside of the tent that the show was being disturbed. A large, burly man seated in the front row arose and left the tent. The profanity stopped and the man returned to his seat. Quiet reigned during the rest of the performance. I did not know what had happened, but I was later informed that the husky man had given the Indian a punch in the jaw which had rendered him unconscious for a couple of hours.

Some boys spread a report that they were going to explode a bomb under the hall on the last night of the show. This frightened a few people, who remained at home that night. The ones who attended were somewhat nervous. When the show was half over, the electric lights suddenly increased to a terrific brilliancy and then were extinguished, while a loud noise came from some unknown quarter. The total darkness produced a panic; children cried, women screamed, men shouted, and a general pandemonium prevailed. As no one was injured, quiet was soon restored. The trouble was caused by a faulty governor on my electric light plant. This broke and caused the engine to race, which increased the power of the voltage, which in turn burned out the incandescent lights.

In a southern community, I was warned that a gang of would-be toughs were going to come to the tent grounds during the night and cut the guy ropes. As my wife and I slept in the house trailer with no one else around, this situation was not conducive to a good night's rest. However, nothing happened. The next morning, a man asked me how I'd gotten along during the night. I told him that I was somewhat nervous, as we were there alone and could not have done much to protect ourselves in case it became necessary. The man smiled and said, "You all wasn't alone. You see them two trees yonder, and that shed? There was one of us men with a shotgun behind each o'them, and if them fellers had a'tried to do anything, we'd a'shot 'em flat on the ground. We watched 'till sun up." So during the night, I had the protection of three guardian angels. The fact that they were not the spiritual kind with harps, wings, and halos mattered very little. Shotguns are more practical in a case of this kind.

If I had any real opposition at all, it usually came from local affairs. When a show came to town, someone would be sure to start some activity which depended on public attendance for its success. One favorite opposition project was a series of home parties. As parties collected no admission fee, they were well-attended. Sometimes the churches started revival meetings. There were also unplanned events which influenced my attendance. A death in the town would have a perceptible effect. A wedding celebration did not help any. An oyster supper at a lodge hall was another loss. Dances took a large number of my paying customers. Rehearsals for home talent plays and graduation exercises were a pain in the neck. But in spite of all opposition I plugged along.

Other small shows hardly ever interfered with me, but the times they tried, I could always get the best of them There were many ways of doing it. If I was showing in a town for a week and a one-night show billed against me, I would publicly announce that on Thursday night (their date), I would give my total door receipts to the Red Cross Fund or to some other charitable organization. When Thursday arrived, the opposition show would not sell a single ticket. Probably the nastiest trick I ever played on a competitor happened in the East. I was staying all winter in a small town and giving a show in what once had been a motion picture theatre. I was drawing good crowds, when some other picture exhibitor heard about it and booked his show for one night a week against me. As the little town did not have a population sufficiently large to support two shows, I had to eliminate my opponent. This I easily did, although not in a manner strictly in accord with professional ethics. The theater was still equipped with a motion picture projection machine. In order to project a bright picture, the lens of the machine had to be crystal clear. My competition used this house machine. To prevent him from getting a bright, clear picture, I dirtied the lens. He did not know enough to examine the lens and clean it. His picture was dim, and the public would not attend his show. So he quit. I believe this to be the worst misdeed of my life. Am I sorry? I just wouldn't know.

When the silent pictures first appeared they were the strongest kind of opposition. There were none in the places where I was showing, but country folk would drive miles to the nearest large town to attend them. I easily overcame this problem by acquiring a machine and films of my own and adding movies to my already satisfactory show. The public liked pictures, especially the comic ones. I had an unusually good comedy at one time. The picture machine I had was one of the first on the market, and it had to be cranked by hand. One night, I delegated this duty to one of the young girls with the show. I had forgotten to rewind the film after the last show, and the picture appeared upside down on the screen. People were on their heads, walking backwards, etc. Everybody started laughing. To make matters worse, the girl operator was struck with the humor of the situation. She laughed so violently that she lost control of her actions and moved the projector so that part of the picture was off the screen. The girl's laughter changed to a guffaw, and the more she guffawed, the more she moved the machine, and the worse the picture became. The picture finally came to an end. After the show a man told me it was the best comedy he had ever seen.

I never thought of myself as being a great magician, musician or ventriloquist. I did, however, consider my show as a whole as being good, and my ability as a magician sufficiently meritorious so that I could present it anywhere, in any town, large or small. While most of my activities were in the smaller places, I did occasionally entertain in the largest of cities and always received excellent comments. As a small town attraction, I believe my show to have been the best in the world. I base my belief on the opinions of many persons who were experienced in such matters. Probably the most satisfactory recommendation I ever had was from a farmer in the Midwest. When he was a young man his father died, and he inherited from him a large farm and about $25,000 in cash. He used the money to take a trip around the world. He came home broke and went to work on his farm. He said, "I have been in the largest cities of the world and have seen many good shows. In Paris I paid the equivalent of ten dollars for a seat in a theatre. I saw many shows much larger and better than yours, but I can't say that I enjoyed any of them any more than I did your little show, which cost me ten cents."

I was a versatile performer and had hundreds of small magical tricks which were suitable for stage performances and numerous large illusions. I had several shows, all different. My best attraction was a levitation act with a hypnotized lady floating about the stage. Next best was a sensational trunk escape. Then came a spiritualistic act about which there was nothing spiritual, though many believed it to be genuine spiritualism. In fact, one man so believed in my spiritualistic powers that he wanted me to give him the power to cause his divorced wife to disappear. (I told him that I could impart no such gift, but advised him that if he would face the east each night and morning and repeat the Lord's Prayer ten times for a year, some such power might come to him.) I had a black art effect, in which act the whole stage was draped with black velvet. The performer and all apparatus were white. The remarkable effects produced in this act are difficult to describe. I seldom used black art, however; stages were too small.

The bullet-catching act had the best advertising possibilities, and it was the most exciting trick I did. I would allow a stranger from the audience to mark the bullet of a cartridge, place it in a rifle, aim, and shoot at me. I would catch the marked bullet between my teeth. While the effect was accomplished by trickery, there was a certain amount of danger connected with it. After I had placed the marksman at the rear of the hall I had to walk to the stage. I could not see what he was doing, and he had a chance to do something to interfere with the success of the trick. At one time, the shooter dropped the blade of a small penknife into the barrel of the rifle. The blade did not fit the barrel tightly, and so it did not carry far or with precision. I caught the marked bullet. At another time the marksman put a few shoe buttons into the barrel. They rattled harmlessly around me; and again I caught the bullet. Then a friend of mine was killed in London while doing the same trick. I decided it was time to discontinue this dangerous money-making attraction.

Besides my mystery effects, I had other means of entertainment. I had illustrated songs, which were highly popular at that period. My wife, Mabel, did a spectacular serpentine dance. There were novelty musical instruments, such as musical glasses, Swiss bells, china bowls, bottles, xylophone, cow bells, organ pipes, and others. I had a Punch and Judy show (the standard, old-time English version of that act), and crayon and rag pictures. There was a circus marionette show which included a ball juggler, a contortionist, a bar juggler, a tumbler, and a trapeze artist, as well as a clown and a trick mule. I also had chapeaugraphy, and mind reading tricks, etc. The main attractions for the children were the puppets and the ventriloquist act, with a dummy whose stage name was Shorty (family name unknown). When I acquired the picture machine, I would add on a two-reel comedy to each of the programs, or one night I might have an all picture show like "Uncle Tom's Cabin" or "Life of Christ." I did not adhere strictly to a definite schedule. I could safely advertise that I had more to entertain with than any other one person in the world. My claim was never challenged.

The ventriloquist act was a riot, the dummy getting all the credit. He appeared to be so real that the children actually believed him to be alive. They would bring candy to him or want him to come out and play with them. One little boy wanted to know why he did not attend school. When the children had afternoon parties, Shorty was sure to be invited. A little girl came with a sleigh and wanted to take him for a ride. A small boy wanted him to come and sleep with him some night. I strongly felt that the children's parents were responsible for some of these notions.

Several times I found myself in difficulties on account of my ventriloquial ability. In a hotel operated by some immigrants, a young girl knocked on my door every morning to awaken me for breakfast. She wore wooden-soled shoes, and I could hear her clap clapping down the hall before she knocked. One morning when she knocked, I answered in a feminine voice, "All right," and then, in my own voice, I said, "Don't say anything to let them know you are in here." Clap, clap, clap down the hall she ran, down the stairs to say to her mother, "Mama, that showman's got a woman in his room." It took a lot of explaining to get me out of that predicament. On one occasion I took my dummy to my hotel room to do some practicing after the show. The landlord, hearing two people speaking in a room where there should be only one person, thought that I was surreptitiously taking someone into my room to spend the night. He demanded an explanation. He got it. These two incidents occurred at a time when my wife was away on a visit. One cold, blizzardy night, the train was late. In the railroad station were a number of people who had been waiting for the train for hours, my wife and myself being two of them. Just for a joke, I imitated the sound of an engine whistle. Instantly, about twenty people grabbed luggage and went out into the storm. The train did not show up, so they returned to the waiting room. In a short time I repeated the performance and there was another exodus into the storm. I tried it the third time, and someone discovered the hoax. I am lucky to be alive to tell about it.

While I could fool adults and children with my assumed voices, I could not fool a little dog. I made Shorty call him by name and speak to him in other ways. All the dog would do was look at my mouth and wag his tail, paying no attention to Shorty's mouth movement. I tried the same experiment with a very young child with the same results.

I also could not fool police authorities at the time the Lindbergh baby was abducted. There was intense excitement throughout the nation. Highway police were stopping and searching automobiles carrying children in an effort to find the missing child. I was making a long Sunday drive from West Virginia to Michigan. I started out early in the morning with a car and trailer. The dummy was bundled in a rather slovenly manner in a piece of canvas with the shoe-covered feet in view. The bundle had all the appearance of a bundled up child. The thought occurred to me that the police along the route might stop me to investigate the bundle. Then I thought it would be a lot of fun if they did. I rearranged the package to place the feet in a very conspicuous position. Every time I stopped for gasoline or for a meal I expected someone to notice the suspicious looking parcel and notify the police. As soon as I was on my way I expected to hear the sirens of chasing police cars. I made a 450 mile journey without having anyone even notice the deceptive bait.

The townspeople were always affected by my show. In one place, a mother went out into the yard and found her little boy shooting into a bucket of water with his air rifle. "What on earth are you trying to do?" she asked. The little boy answered, "I been a-shootin' in this bucket o' water all morning, and I can't make no ducks come out like that man did in the show last night." Another little boy said to me, grinning, "Mister, you got a show?" I said, "Yes." "You gotta clown?" was the next question. As country people always termed a comedian a clown, I answered, "Yes, we have a clown." He looked suspicious, and said, "The last show that was here claimed they had one, but after they wuz gone we found out that it wuz just one of their own people painted up."

One amusing incident happened in presenting my Aerial Suspension Illusion. I always pretended to hypnotize the lady first, but on a few occasions I pretended to render her unconscious by having her inhale ether fumes from a handkerchief applied to her nostrils. As this had no advantage over the hypnotic method, I went back to that. While I was using "ether," I once heard a peculiar remark. Two women were engaged in conversation. One of them said, "Do you know I got sick at the show last night. When that man used ether to put that woman to sleep I could smell it away out in the audience and I got sick in my stomach and had to go home. I never could stand the smell of ether." The ether I used was water.

Sometimes the joke was on me. During a conversation with an old lady, she told me that her grandson was a good musician. I asked what instrument he played, and she said that he played a horn. When I asked what kind of music he played, she said that he played any kind, and also that he could sing any kind of songs. This seemed to be something quite unusual for a young country boy to be able to do in those days, so I asked the others about him and discovered that the boy had a phonograph, and the horn he played was the amplifying horn of that old-time, versatile noise-making instrument. One time I did the restored card minus the corner trick. I gave the corner to a man to hold, thinking I would regain it in some mysterious manner. He forestalled that by chewing the corner and swallowing it.

Tricks hardly ever went wrong for me. When they did, fortunate happenings got me out of my predicament. I was in the middle of a decided failure when a blinding flash of lightning and a tremendous crash of thunder shook the building and bewildered the audience for a moment. By the time they had recovered their equanimity, I had made some necessary adjustments in my apparatus. At another time, a woman fainted and fell in the aisle. This caused a delay in the performance and saved my reputation. At one time, I squirmed out of a bad dilemma while the electric lights were out for a moment.

After the show I packed up everything. I showed in the tent, and if there was a bad storm or a blow down during the night, everything not in the trunks would be damaged by water. So I packed up everything every night. Next, I had to tip all the wall poles around the tent to allow, as I have stated, for the rope shrinkage during the night. While doing this, I discovered a drunken man lying on the ground near the side wall. He was dead to the world, and I could not awaken him. Someone told me that he was an Indian lumberjack, living in a boarding house a couple of miles away. As I did not care to have him in the tent overnight, I raised the canvas, rolled him over twice, and he was outside the tent. I went into the house trailer where my wife had a lunch prepared. After eating, I shut off the light plant and it was dark. Illumination from now on would be by coal lantern. It was 11 p.m., and I had been active since 7:30 a.m. I was ready to crawl into bed.

At about one a.m., it started raining. As I did not like the idea of anyone lying on the ground with rain falling on him, I rose and rolled the Indian back into the shelter of the big tent. At about three a.m. he became conscious and, not knowing just where he was, he screamed and swore and raised a general disturbance. I rose again and managed to get him into a small wagon borrowed from a neighbor at that unearthly hour, and with the aid of a horse hauled him home. It was daylight when I finally got to bed again, and I went peacefully to sleep, knowing I had done my good deed for that day or night.

Moving day came once a week, but when it did come, it was a day of about eighteen hours of work. As the tent season was also the summer season, the day was not only long, it was also hot. I never had horses of my own, but always hired men with horses to do the moving. In later years I had auto-trucks and a trailer house. I needed three men, three teams of horses, and three large platform or dray wagons. My agreement with the men was that they were to take down the tent and load it and everything else on the wagons, take everything to the next town, erect the tent, place all property in the proper place, and erect the stage and seats. I promised that this would not take more than two hours.

Moving day consisted of a series of undesirable events, the first of which was the arising hour. This was at five a.m., as we had to have an hour's time to have breakfast and be ready for the movers when they arrived. Usually they were late. The first thing they did was to load the thirty trunks of magical apparatus on one of the wagons. This constituted one load. Next, they placed the stage flooring and supports, seat planks and jacks on the second wagon. This was piled so as to keep the load flat. On top of these, they placed the tent after taking it down and rolling it into a large bundle. To take down the tent they had to remove the center poles, then the wall poles. This left the top flat on the ground. The ropes had to be untied and removed from the stakes. If they were wet, this was no easy matter. After the struggle to untie the ropes, the stakes had to be pulled. If the ground was dry, and it usually was, this was a backbreaking job even with a lever stake puller. When all of this was put on the second wagon, that load was complete. The third load consisted of the living tent and its contents. When the three loads were completed, they had to be roped to prevent the articles from shifting and falling off. The outfit was now ready to start on a ten-mile trip over rough country roads.

The loads were heavy and the horses could not go faster than two and a half miles an hour. My wife and I went ahead in a horse and buggy belonging to one of the movers. We could get to our destination in about two and one half hours. Moving at that slow pace, through dust and heat, was not conducive to the development of the love for show business. If there was no eating place in town we had to take along a lunch and eat it, picnic fashion, under a tree (that is if there was a tree). Then came a long, tiresome wait for the loads to arrive. Sometimes there was a delay because the wagon broke down on account of the heavy load, or the horses became exhausted because of the excessive heat, or sometimes because the men stopped too many times at saloons along the way. By some hook or crook, they always managed to arrive dusty and hungry.

After a rest, the erection of the outfit began. The living tent was put up first. Next came the big tent. It had to be unrolled and unfolded until it was flat on the ground. About forty stakes, three feet long, had to be driven. A guy rope had to be tied to each stake. As farmers had no knowledge of a rope tie called the circus hitch, I had to do the tying. The hempen ropes were rough and as my hands were tender, I usually had blisters on them when the job was finished. This put them in fine condition for manipulative magic. Next, the wall poles were placed in position. Then the center poles raised the top so that there was a sloppy looking tent in the air. This had to be trued up by adjusting every rope to its proper length and tension. To do this I had to untie all the knots, adjust the ropes and retie them. This was another punishment to my tender hands. After the seats and stage had been erected and the side wall put in place, I was ready to pay the men and send them home. Minor items like stage curtains and lighting equipment, I attended to myself. Although the men did all of the work I had to direct them, and I was completely exhausted after an eighteen hour day of activity. But I had a nice tent theater and would be ready to stand at the door the next night and collect money and give shows.

Did you ever try to conduct a small tent show single-handed? You probably did not, as not many persons in their right mind would be idiotic enough to attempt such a thing. I did and did it for nearly fifty years, and have survived the ordeal, and am able to write about it.

Because I gave my performance under canvas, as show people say, the summer season was always the most profitable for me. Since I had good outdoor equipment, this was really the ideal way to work. For seven months I would live out-of-doors and breath only pure air. There were no dirty halls or ignorant hall managers and janitors to contend with. A tent is always attractive and alluring, and people will go to one when they would not go into a building, especially the kind of building I otherwise showed in. The white canvas and green grass is a pleasing color combination. Even my electric light plant was a big attraction. This being before electric service became common in the country, the plant had almost as much drawing power as the tent and show.

I could put up the tent wherever I could find a piece of ground, so that I did not have to depend on a village. If need be, I could put the tent on a farm and depend on the patronage of the surrounding farmers. Some residents of villages would object to having a tent show near their homes, but on the other hand, some of them welcomed it. In one town, the local clergyman allowed me to place the tent on the church lawn. The stakes and guy ropes were so close to the church door that the worshippers had to step over them to gain entrance on Sunday morning. One time my tent was on a pasture lot surrounded by a cattle fence. A little boy stood looking at the fence and the tent and the gate, and said to another boy, "I wonder how they ever got that big tent through such a narrow gate." On some quiet summer night, with scarcely a movement of the tree leaves and a stillness that seemed to proclaim peace and serenity with the whole world, suddenly there would be an ominous rumble at the distant horizon. Instantly, all thoughts of peace and serenity disappeared, and excitement and confusion took their place. There was a storm approaching. I would run around like a chicken with its head cut off, not knowing which way to turn or what to do first. Generally, my concern was to see that there was no opening on the windward side of the tent for the wind to enter and raise the whole tent off the ground. Then I had to close all other openings. The lightning flashes were brighter and more frequent, the thunder claps were louder, and a few rain drops were falling. By the time I had the ropes of the small tent tightened, the storm was on full force with a heavy wind and a deluging rain. I was out in it all with my eyes on the big tent, which was billowing like a huge ocean wave. Lightening struck a tree a few hundred feet away and I could feel the shock. I saw that some of the stakes of the big tent were loosening. I was drenched to the skin, but I did not dare neglect the tent and seek shelter. I grabbed a thirteen-pound maul and drove in the loosening stakes. As soon as I had one stake down in the ground, another one or two loosened. I tightened these. I was out of breath, soaking wet, and panting with exhaustion. More stakes were loosening, and it seemed as though the tent might go over at any moment. Then the force of wind lessened, the thunder and lightening became less frequent, and the rain stopped. In a few minutes the storm was over. The tent was still up, although somewhat lopsided. About this time, a man would come from a neighboring house and ask if I needed help. The tent would be lopsided until morning, when it would have to be lined up.

A storm like this did no great amount of damage to property, but it was a heavy drain on my vitality and nervous energy. Sometimes there was a different finish to the storm. I would not be able to keep the stakes in the ground, and an unusually strong gust of wind would pull them all out at one time. The tent would go down and be torn in a dozen places. Everything not in trunks would be damaged by water. I lost about one hundred books on magic in this manner. The next few days would find me sitting in the hot sun in an open field, repairing the tent. There was no one who could be hired to do this work. Handling rough canvas and sewing with large needles and heavy twine did not improve the condition of my hands either. In a couple of days the tent would be back in service again, and I would have forgotten all about the storm. During the many years in which I conducted a tent show, I had six tents destroyed by wind storms. But in spite of all the work, the trouble, and the nerve-racking experiences, etc., I liked the tent.

I always stayed in the tent until cold weather stopped me. When the night temperature dropped to near freezing, I tried to heat the tent. I was told that burning coke would not give off smoke and that I could burn it in an open stove without a chimney. As this sounded good, I arranged a container in which to burn coke. I had been correctly informed. It did not give off any smoke, but it did give off irritating gas fumes which caused everyone in the audience to cough and sneeze. Some became nauseated. I refunded all admission money and the next day I stored my tent, or, in show parlance, I went in the barn.

After closing the tent season, I usually worked a few places in halls. This would be in the fall of the year when the farmers still had money left from the sales of summer produce. As soon as reduced door receipts warned me that they were running out of money I stored the greater part of my elaborate outfit and, with a couple of suitcases, headed for the city. Educated city people were easier to entertain than the ignorant country folks of those days. I always enjoyed a six-week (but only six weeks) stay in some city.

Olive Chandler Rapp,

THE ACCOMPLISHED SINGER AND PIANIST,

Will Furnish the MUSICAL PART of the Program.

BIRTH OF THE
American Flag

A Patriotic Trick and one of the Most Expensive Illusions ever produced, MR. RAPP shows his skill in handling large articles by producing from space, a large, pure silk flag, 10 ft. high by 16 ft. long.

SUBSTITUTION

Can a Human Being Dematerialize?
Can Matter Pass Through Matter?

You will think so when you see this Most Bewildering of all Deceptions.

Mind Reading Tests.

In Mind Reading, MR. RAPP excels all others, as he reads the minds of people of your own community. See him locate hidden articles, tell anyone the date of their birth, tell you the names of your dead friends, etc., etc. See him execute

The Book and Needle Test.
The Nail and Hammer Test.
The Playing Card Test.
The Marriage Test.
The Murder Test.

Spiritualism,

Viewed from a Scientific and Religious Standpoint.

Materialization of Hands, Faces and Full Forms

Floating Chairs and Tables.   Trumpet Messages and Spirit Voices.   Slate Writing, with Single, Double and Sealed Slates.

114

CHAPTER SEVEN

MUST BE SPOOKS

Regarding all the controversy concerning spiritualism, I will add my ten cent's worth by saying that I have been mixed in the mess all of my life and have never seen anything which would convince me that there was such a thing as communication with the dead. I have seen supposed mediums give tests which were hanky panky tricks not worth looking at, but which converted men and women to a positive belief in man's ability to communicate with the spirits. I made every effort to obtain a test for myself which I could consider genuine, because if there was such a thing as real mediumship, I wanted to become a medium.

Consultation long ago was only a dollar. I visited many mediums and hinted that I would like to receive a message from a dead wife (this was before I was married). In every instance, I received the desired message. When I told one medium that I had never had a wife, she said that this message was from a wife in the spirit land, of whose existence I was not aware. I started wondering how many more wives I might have in the spirit land, and if it was illegal to commit spiritualistic bigamy. I also wondered why, if spirits wished to talk to us, they always selected an uncouth and ignorant person to act as their medium. Why did they have to work in the dark, knock on walls and foot boards of bedsteads, ring bells, thump tambourines, and do other ridiculous things to manifest their presence, and then run away? Why did they not select some intelligent man or woman and communicate something of value, like a specific cure for some dreaded disease?

I have not heard these questions answered. In my opinion, the reason that a medium is always an ignorant person is that an intelligent person would not have the nerve to practice such apparent deceptions. The subject of spirit communication is still a debatable one. With improved methods of investigation being developed, future experiments by more qualified persons along this line may be more conclusive.

During the first two decades of the twentieth century spiritualism flourished both as a religious belief and as a means of earning money fraudulently. Spiritualistic churches with supposedly qualified ministers came into existence from no one knew where. No one seemed to know how the "reverends" received the education which qualified them to preach the gospel and to order the collection box to be passed around. I had proof that they could have a diploma certifying their fitness to be whatever they wanted. I was able to secure a diploma proclaiming me to be an ordained minister of the spiritualistic church. I did not have to go to college and study to obtain this degree. All I needed to do was to pay twenty–five dollars. I purchased one to keep as a curiosity, but it was destroyed in the fire. Later, I discovered that bargain diplomas could be purchased for as little as five dollars, very much like the fraudulent medical diplomas of those days. Such a diploma made a great impression on those interested in spiritualism and its possibilities and services. The main disadvantage of this belief was that for many years it enabled charlatans to earn a living. They gave a public seance in small halls on Sunday night, under the cloak of a religious service to advertise their private readings during the week. The public seances were advertised as free, but the usual donation basket was always in evidence. The seance commenced with a prayer. Then there was a song or two. A favorite song was:

I have a mother in the spirit land,
I have a mother in the spirit land,
When my mother calls me, I will go,
To meet her in the spirit land.

I have a father in the spirit land,
I have a father in the spirit land,
When my father calls me, I will go,
To meet him in the spirit land.

This was sung followed by brothers, sisters, cousins, aunts, and as many relatives as they could think they might have in the spirit land concluding with:

We all have friends in the spirit land, etc.

The air of the song was different every time I heard it. The persons in the meeting were seated in an oval with the medium at one end. To work properly, the medium had to go into a trance. To get into this condition she (most mediums were women) closed her eyes, grunted a few grunts, and made a few body movements which would lead one to believe she was trying to avoid belching or might have a bellyache. These contortions were supposed to place her in another world or bring the other world to her, where she could contact spirits. Now she was ready to give tests.

Tests were supposed to be proofs of the medium's ability to communicate with the spirits. Verbal messages from spirits to members in the audience were generally given. Here is a sample of what they were like. In a weak, sickly, assumed voice, she might say, "I see a woman, a very young woman, who is asking for her mother. She says her name is Carrie. Is there anyone present who has a deceased daughter named Carrie?" If no one acknowledged the spirit, the medium would contort some more and continue, "It seems I am mistaken about the name Carrie; it is Mary. Does anyone have a spirit daughter named Mary?" If no one answered she would pretend to hear someone say "yes," and continue with, "Your daughter Mary sends love and asks me to tell you she is happy and waiting for the day when you will come and join her." About the only information ever received from the spirits was that they were happy. Every medium had a different way of giving a show. Experienced mediums would have a big selection of tests to pick from. Most of them also had special information about the sitters which was obtained in advance. They also had an accomplice or two in the circle who would acknowledge any message the medium might give. When the medium ran out of tests she would falter, stutter, and whisper to give the impression of a weak ghost, and find it necessary to stop. Then she would return to normal.

Those verbal messages were given in full light. Physical manifestations were just what the name implies, efforts of the spirits to manifest their presence by physical methods. These seances had to take place in the dark, partly because spirits are visible only in the dark, but mostly to prevent the sitters from discovering the *modus operandi.* In these seances the medium's hands were always held by the adjacent sitters, who would swear on a stack of ten-cent-store Bibles that she did not move. Inside of the circle of sitters were placed the articles needed to give the demonstration. There was always a tea bell or two, a cow bell and a tambourine. Just why spirits had a liking for small bells and tambourines is a mystery I have never been able to solve, but they did. There would be a slender megaphone through which the spirits could talk; the belief being that as they were weak (probably undernour-ished), they could not talk very loud and needed the mega-phone to amplify the voice sounds. The truth was that if something was not used to change or disguise the voice, the source would be recognized. The megaphone was called a trumpet, and the communications were trumpet messages. Usually there was also a guitar and a mouth organ.

When the lights were extinguished, there was usually a song to help to make the show last a sufficient length of time. Generally the bells and tambourines would tinkle first. They would float around and touch sitters on the head, or they might be violently thrown out of the circle. A voice would come through the trumpet giving the message. The guitar would be strummed and a tune would be played on the mouth organ.

Spirit lights and faintly luminous objects would float about. A star would indicate fortune; a horse shoe, luck; an anchor, hope. Sometimes something resembling a face would move about. This would always be recognized as being that of a relative of one of the sitters. Sometimes more than one person would claim the face. This worthless, insignificant performance made a deep impression on most of those who attended. They would file silently out past the contribution box and give for the support of the cause : the medium. Before leaving, they would be notified where and when they could have a private sitting. The various effects produced in the circle were not done by the medium. They were produced by her helpers in the circle who were supposed to be *bona fide* sitters. The lights were cardboard, painted with luminous paint which was not generally known at that time. A luminous spot of any kind might be recognized by different persons as different things.

Private sittings were usually given at the medium's home. Here, on payment of a fee (always a fee), she would do or tell almost anything. She was able to diagnose disease, to heal, give advice on personal affairs, predict events, locate missing persons, find lost articles, get messages from spirits, photograph spirits, and even materialize spirits so they could be seen. By looking into a crystal ball she could tell everything she did or did not see. The first spirit photographs were double exposures. Then it was discovered that forms, faces, etc, painted on a background with a certain chemical would be invisible to the eye, but would have an effect on a sensitized photographic plate. A person photographed before this prepared background would have the forms or faces appear on the photo with him. These would be indistinct, but would be recognized as someone. When this method became known to the public, spirit photos went out of style. The appearance of a full-sized spirit was also easy to manage. One of the accomplices carried a couple of yards of gauze, also treated with luminous paint. By holding this cloth in his hand, he could make it look somewhat like a spirit. That is, if anyone knew what spirit looked like. The spirit of a child was

119

produced by holding the gauze at the height of a child above the floor.

Some mediums had more elaborate seances than the one just described. One man had a house built with secret panels in the walls which could be opened for the admission of helpers. There were also a trap door in the ceiling and special electric wiring, with a view to deceive and fool the suckers, as the mediums called their patrons. One well-known medium specialized in securing marriage partners for those who wanted to find a spouse when they got to the spirit land. The prospective bride or bridegroom had to furnish plenty of money, supposedly to finance the wedding necessities. About the time the wedding was to have taken place, the medium and the money would disappear. Many mediums were exposed as tricksters, but this did not seem to diminish the faith of the faithful.

Any efficient magician can duplicate all the so–called tests offered by so-called mediums. Magicians can also show quasi-spirit tests which are more remarkable than those done by the fraudulent mediums. I have used these anti-spiritualistic effects in my show for over half a century and have obtained results so marvelous that I almost became a convert myself. I said almost. The lamentable fact was that many believers would not accept as truth my statements that all of my effects were the result of trickery or deception of some kind. They said I was a genuine medium masquerading as a magician, that I wanted to build myself a reputation as a skillful wizard and was unwilling to give credit to the unseen world for my powers. They were naming me just what I named them, liars. It did not worry me as much as it did them, because the shoe did not pinch me so hard as it did them.

One of the most puzzling performances I gave was my Spirit Cabinet Act. The name was as near as it came to having anything to do with spirits, and I so advertised the fact. But the effects of the act were so remarkable that many credulous persons were converted to a spiritualistic belief. To the audience it looked like this.

The stage setting consisted of a large, black cabinet. This was an enclosure about six-feet-square, made of black cloth, with a sliding front curtain. Cabinet is hardly the proper name for it. It probably was so called because some of the first spiritualistic manifestations were given in a wooden cabinet and the name continued in use. The front curtain had a square opening or window which was covered by a small curtain hanging at its upper edge. The cloth cabinet was either supported by an iron framework or was suspended from ropes. The front curtain was arranged so as to slide open easily and show the interior of the enclosure. Two chairs for use by the committee men were placed one at each front corner of the stage. After a few introductory remarks, I would ask for two gentlemen from the audience to act as a committee to examine everything I used and to be able to state that none of the articles I used were prepared in any way. They were to satisfy themselves that no one could be concealed in the cabinet, and also that there was no trap door in the stage through which a person might enter. I was very particular about this because the usual explanation of the act by those who did not believe in spirits was that I had hidden assistance, that someone was able to quickly enter and leave the cabinet without being detected.

Next, I showed a piece of two-by-four lumber which was four feet long. This had a one-foot piece of one-inch board nailed across its bottom so it could be nailed to the floor and thus form a substantial post. With a brace and bit, one of the men bored three one-inch holes through the two by four. When I was seated in front of the post, the upper hole would be opposite my neck. Below this would be a hole opposite my elbows, and the lower hole would be near my wrists when I had my hands tied behind me. The men nailed the post to the stage floor at the rear of the inside of the cabinet. In front of this they placed a folding camp seat.

Next, I showed a yard of unbleached muslin, which I tore into a number of strips. I would give one to the man on my right and ask him to tie it tightly around my right wrist. The man on my left would tie a strip around that wrist. With adhesive tape they fastened the bandages to my skin. To prevent the knots from being converted into slip knots, the men would sew through all the knots with a needle and black thread. Bandages were tied around my arms at the elbows and around my neck. Next, my hands were tied together behind me. I seated myself, in this condition, on the camp seat in front of the post. The men then fastened me to the post. They passed the neck bandage through the hole in the post, drew me back against it, and knotted the bandage. The arms and wrists were fastened in a similar manner. Finally, all of the ends of the bandages were nailed to the post with tacks. I was now securely trussed up against the post. I was not capable of making a movement of any kind. My head, elbows, and wrists could not move away from the post. My feet were not tied, as they were always sticking out from under the front curtain when it was closed, so that they could always be seen by the audience. The committee was then asked to be seated on the chairs.

I would then offer a number of tests to prove the presence of some unseen power. I never designated what power; just an unseen power. This was a sensational performance mostly on account of its rapidity. There was no chance for outside assistance. There was no second person concealed in the cabinet. There was no chance for concealed mechanism. I was unable to do the work, so there was no explanation other than that of "spirits" to the faithful who wanted to have it that way.

Test 1

My assistant, usually a lady, would put a small tea bell in a tambourine and place them in a cabinet. She would close the curtain with my feet sticking out from underneath it. She would retain a hold on the curtain so she could open it instantly. The moment the curtain was closed and I was screened from view, the bell would sound and the tambourine would rattle as though someone was shaking and hitting it.

122

While the sounds were continuing I would loudly call out, "Lights." In less than a second the assistant would pull the curtain aside, sometimes before the instruments had fallen to the floor. As quickly as they could, the committee men would rush into the cabinet and examine all of the fastenings. They were always found to be intact.

Test 2

For this test, several cow bells, the tea bell and the tambourine were used. As soon as the curtain was closed, the din was terrific. At the command of "Lights," the curtain would be quickly opened and the bells would be seen dropping to the floor. There was no time for even a spirit to enter and leave, and there was no time for me to even try to make a move. After each test the committee would examine the fastenings, and they would always be found to be undisturbed.

Test 3

For this test I used a borrowed ring. One of the committee would place it in the cabinet and the curtain would be quickly closed. Before he could reach his chair to be seated, the committee man would hear the cry of "Lights." He would return and be told to hunt for the ring. When he was unable to find it, I would tell him to remove it from my right ear and return it to its owner.

Test 4

This time I used a mouth organ. I would take a mouthful of water and have the mouth organ placed in the cabinet. The curtain would be closed. Instantly, mouth organ music would be coming from the cabinet. I could not call out "Lights" as my mouth was filled with water. I would make a sound like a rough grunt. The lady assistant would know that it meant to open the curtain, and she quickly did so. On examination, my mouth was still filled with water. As proof of the fact I had to spit it on the floor. Everything was examined again.

Test 5

For this test, one of the committee removed his coat and laid it on my lap. Again, the curtain was closed. In just a few seconds the "Lights" cry would be heard. When the curtain was opened, I was seen to be wearing the borrowed coat and my own coat on my lap. And again there was a rigid examination.

Test 6

This time a sharp table knife was placed in the cabinet with me. In an incredibly short time, the signal "Lights" was heard again. This time the opened curtain showed me released from the post with all of the bandages cut. The knots were still sewed with the black thread and the bandages were still fastened to my wrists by the adhesive tape.

Of course, there always were those hard-headed skeptics who had ideas of their own as to how the act might have been done. Some thought I had a small monkey concealed under my clothing who did the work. This would be an ideal explanation if one could always find a monkey that could play a mouth organ. Others were sure I shoved my slippers out under the curtain and slipped my feet out of them to do the work. This would also be a fine way to do it, but for the fact that I wore laced shoes and I am not limber or skillful enough to put a ring in my ear with my toes. At one time the committee became so excited over the performance that they tore the cabinet cloth to shreds in an endeavor to locate something that I might have concealed therein. Of course they discovered nothing. The next day I received an anonymous letter containing money to be used in replacing the damaged cabinet cloth. I believe that I fooled a million people with this performance. A noted woman medium travelled and fooled scientists all over the world with it. The secret of the act was a very simple one, but it took many years of practice before I could perform it as skillfully as I have described. Also, its successful execution depended to a large extent on a skillful and alert assistant, and such are extremely hard to find.

All seances I gave were the imitation kind, but the most remarkable happenings occurred sometimes, as this experience will prove. While I was tied hands and feet in the spirit cabinet, spirits and flowers would materialize and come out of the cabinet in a very dim light. As usual I had members of the audience seated on the stage to act as a committee to see that there was no deception, or to detect if there was. I do not know of what value these committees were, unless it was to give an impression of veracity and fair play. Of the many thousands of them I had on my stage, none ever discovered anything; or if they did, they never mentioned it. On this occasion, one of the committee members was a very stout woman who lived two miles out in the country. After various minor manifestations such as lights and hands and faces appearing and moving about, a small child had presented the woman with a bouquet of flowers. She recognized the spirit as that of a deceased daughter and wept hysterically. This created a sensation among the spectators, but the best was yet to come. The next morning the woman came to town via horse and buggy, frantically clutching the flowers and possessing positive proof that the spirit was that of her daughter. She said, "Now I am positive that was my little girl, because she picked the flowers from my own garden. I fitted the broken ends of the bouquet stalks to the stalks in my garden, and they matched exactly." Compared to this miracle, any magic trick I ever did paled into insignificance.

Here is how it happened. I wanted to produce some flowers during the seance. There was no place in a country village where flowers could be purchased. I gave a small boy a quarter to get some home garden flowers from wherever he could find them, and to sneak them into the show hall. He took his bicycle out into the country, noticed that no one was at home at a farm house, and went into the garden and helped himself to a generous amount of flowers. It just so happened that the stout lady with the deceased daughter lived on the farm. This test created great excitement in that locality, until the little boy told how and where I obtained the flowers. By that time I had left the place, and the story could not follow me to the next town because telephone communication was not highly developed, and autos were non-existent.

No less marvelous was the sealed slate test. I would allow patrons to bring slates tied together with string or tape. The knots could be sealed with sealing wax. The slates would be placed in the cabinet with me for a moment and then returned to the person who brought them. The seals on the knots would be unbroken. When the slates were separated, there would be writing on the inside, supposedly done by some spirit. I was the spirit who did the writing. The method I used was a very old one used by swindling mediums to fool their dupes. The string or tape with which the slates were tied could be stretched slightly. By inserting four small wooden wedges between the slates, they could be separated about an eighth of an inch. A wire with a bit of a pencil fastened to one end of it could be inserted between the slates and used to write a word or short sentence. When the wedges were removed, the tension of the binding string would pull the slates together. This was always a satisfactory test of my mediumistic powers.

On one occasion I managed to get more than a mere word or short sentence. An old lady brought a pair of slates, unusually securely tied. I could hardly insert the wedges between the slates, and they were separated so little that it was difficult to manipulate the wire and pencil. Not wishing to hand the slates back with no writing, I moved the wire and pencil circularly, up and down and back and forth, hoping the lady would believe the scratch to be the unsuccessful attempts of the spirit to write a message. When the lady separated the slates, she screamed and said, "Good Lord, here is a picture of the house I was born in, in England!" To add to the mystery, someone circulated a report that the slates had never left the owner's possession. This report was generally believed to be true. One man's slates had a message signed with his dead father's full name. The man said that his father had been dead for so long that no one could possibly remember his given name. He said that I was a total stranger in town and could not possibly know what it was. But I did. I took it off of an old tombstone in the cemetery.

Equally dumbfounding was my being able to obtain a message between two slates which were tightly bound with wire. The places where the wire crossed were soldered. The slates were then placed in a large paper envelope which was sealed. I got a message and created another sensation. I could not do this good trick at any time, as this informative explanation will make known. In the town in which I was showing was a friend of mine who was an amateur magician. There were also some ardent believers in "spooks." The magician wanted to fool the believers. As he reported to me subsequently, this was his procedure.

He asked one of the believers to help him test my abilities on slate writing. He explained that he was too well-known by the town people as a magician, and if he tried to mix up in the affair they would be suspicious of him, thinking he might be an accomplice of mine. He said he would furnish the slates if the believer would take them to the seance. Together, they would fasten the slates so firmly and securely that it would require tools to pry them apart. This the man agreed to do. The magician brought the slates to the believer's home, and in the basement they worked on the slates. While the believer went upstairs after matches with which to light the blow torch, the magician hastily scribbled a message on one of the slates. He then placed them together with the message inside and started binding them with wire which was soldered at every possible place. The believer brought the slates to the seance (show) but kept them in his possession.

When I saw that he was not going to hand them in, I told

him I would try to get a message anyway. I told him to place the slates against his ear and he would hear noise made by a writing pencil. He did this and said he could not hear anything. I asked him to allow me to listen also. I placed my ear against the other side of the slates. I heard scratching and my listener could also hear sounds. How could we hear the sound of a writing pencil inside the slate? That was another easy trick. When I placed my ear against the slate I gritted my teeth, which sounded like something scratching. It took some rough work to separate the slates, but there was the message. As my magician friend hadn't told me about this, I was as much surprised as anyone. Again I was almost converted.

Much money was fleeced out of gullible people by so-called mediums during the end of the last century by the sealed envelope test or by pretending to be able to read messages or writing of any kind in sealed envelopes. This no one has ever been able to do, but by trickery some very good imitations of it could be done. The first time I saw it done was by a Chinese magician. Many methods have been explained in various books and magical publications. For a long time I used the simplest and oldest method of producing this effect. Then, quite by chance, I hit upon a method which was original and fooled everybody, including magicians.

Briefly, the effect was as follows. A volunteer from the audience was asked to act as an assistant. The man was always a total stranger. He was given a number of small, blank white cards and an equal number of envelopes and pencils. The envelopes were drug envelopes. The cards were square, not oblong. The assistant was told to hand one of each of these to members of the audience. These persons were asked to write something on the cards. They might write a date, a number, a name of a person, a name of a town, or a short sentence. There were to be no questions asked. They were then to place the cards in the envelopes, seal the flaps, and place all in their pockets. I would stand in the center of the stage and, when handed an envelope, hold it about two feet from me, where I could see it. I would then tell, in a loud voice, what was written on the card. The assistant would then return the envelope, unopened, to the person from whom he had taken it.

This person would acknowledge that I was correct in my reading. He could open the envelope and show the card to persons near him, or he could keep the card in the sealed envelope and open it whenever he cared to. I employed no confederates, and the sealed envelopes were brought to me one at a time. I have never divulged the secret of this trick to anyone, and I am not going to do so now. To those who might want to work on this difficult problem, I will say that it is a trick or deception pure and simple, and I will also say that I could not do the trick with oblong instead of square cards. The explanation is so simple that the average person would overlook the method. If it were a complicated matter, there would be something to work with. As it is, the method is so simple that there is no problem to solve.

I did a certain kind of supposed mind reading which had all the earmarks of the genuine article, and believers in spiritualism believed the results were accomplished through spirit agency. It was used principally in finding hidden articles. I showed so-called tests to prove my ability as a mind reader. One was the Murder Test. I would ask for two men from the audience to come on the stage and assist me in my "mental experiments." First, they would cover my eyes with a heavy blindfold so that it would be impossible for me to perceive anything by the sense of sight. I would be seated at the center of the stage with my back to the audience. The men were then instructed to borrow a pocketknife from some person in the audience and to open one blade. Next, they were to select any person to be the murdered man and to touch him with the point of the opened blade as though to stab him. Then the blade was to be closed and the knife was to be hidden somewhere in the hall. They were then to return to the stage for further instructions. While they were doing all of this, I was seated on the stage, blindfolded. As soon as they returned to the stage I would grasp one of them by the hand and ask him to think of the place where they had concealed the knife. I would then lead the way and go to the place where they had hidden the knife and recover it. Then I would change to the second man. He would grasp my wrist and keep his mind on which blade had been used. Immediately I would open that blade. Changing contact to the other man, I would next touch the murdered person with the tip of the blade at the exact spot where he had been "stabbed" by the committee man. Next, I would close the blade, find the owner of the knife, and return it to him.

As a public advertisement, I would give a test on the street known as the Blindfold Street Drive. This test also used a committee which hid articles, but the test was more difficult than most of them. I was heavily blindfolded as usual. Two men would take a large dictionary and a common pin and leave the opera house. After they were out of my sight they were to open the dictionary at any page and select any word. Then they were to get into a horse-drawn surrey and drive anywhere, and hide the pin in one place and the dictionary in another place. They were to drive back to the opera house. While they were gone I was watched so that no one could communicate with me. As soon as they returned I would step into the surrey and be seated on the front seat with a committee man on each side of me holding my wrists. I would take the lines and drive to the spot where the pin had been hidden and find it. Next, I would drive to some other locality and find the dictionary. Then, I would drive back to the opera house. Placing the dictionary on a table, I would thumb through the pages, stop at the selected page, and stick the pin in the selected word. Then I would spell and pronounce the word. As I grew older this performance was too strenuous for me and I finally discontinued it.

When Mabel was a young lady she was an ardent believer in spiritualism. It was going full force at that time. Everything done or said at so-called spirit seances, she believed to be gospel truth, and she accepted their teachings as a basis for a religion. She read many books on the subject. In one of them there was a passage which she could not quite understand. To obtain first-hand knowledge about it she wrote to the author for an explanation. She received a lengthy letter with the information she wanted and a statement saying he would be at a spiritualistic convention to be held in a nearby city. He said if she happened to be there he would be pleased to make her acquaintance and give her further information. She became so excited over an opportunity to meet a celebrated author on spiritualism that she answered immediately saying she would accept his invitation. She purchased new clothing for the occasion and took her mother along as chaperon.

They checked in at a first-class hotel. The author paged and found them. Mabel was somewhat disappointed in his appearance. Instead of the tall, distinguished looking, well-dressed man she expected to see, he was a skinny little runt needing a shave and a haircut. He made arrangements to take them to an evening dinner. When he called for them he was somewhat the worse for liquor. He took them to a very high-class hotel dining room. He ordered intoxicants with the meal and became highly inebriated. Not only that, he spilled his food until his vest was decorated. Also, his words were incoherent, and he wet his pants and water ran in a small stream over the tile floor. I don't know just how the women got rid of him, but I do know that Mabel was cured of wanting to meet high-class writers on spiritualism.

When Mabel and I were married she was still a firm believer in spiritualism and accepted all so-called spiritualistic manifestations as genuine evidences of the spirits being present and being able to communicate with the living. In particular, she was a believer in the performances of Anna Eva Fay. When I explained to her the secret of this vaudeville act, did the same act myself, and taught it to her, she was utterly chagrined. She never again believed in any form of spiritualistic teachings.

I could never understand my wife's remarkable temperamental and constitutional makeup. I know of no name for the kind of a person she was. She seemed to be constituted differently from most people. She was extremely sensitive. If she was in a room and the temperature dropped one degree, she would notice it. If a drop of perfume was placed somewhere in a room during her absence she could, on entering the room, sniff around until she found it. She could do the same with any bit of strong smelling substance, like cheese or a very small piece of spoiled meat. For that reason, I was sure that I would never eat any contaminated foods. If she came in close contact with a person who had a headache, she would immediately acquire the same kind of an ache. The same was true when she came in contact with persons with any other pain or physical disturbance. A person with indigestion would cause her to feel nauseated. One with rheumatism would cause her to have the same kind of a pain. In this way she could diagnose and tell a person of their physical ailments without asking a question.

If she came in contact with a person who would concentrate deeply, she could form a moderately good opinion of what they were thinking about. I do not mean that she could tell, with words, just what was being thought of. She could only describe the subject's thought in a general way. For this reason many people termed her a fortune teller or a spirit medium. She strongly objected to having these two terms used in connection with her name. She did give a character and aptitude reading but disclaimed being able to foretell events or to communicate with spirits. Neither would she accept pay for her readings. Whatever the special faculty was that she possessed, it enabled her to do a fine act as part of my show. It was in the nature of a mental act; at least, it would require two minds to do it, and I would advertise it as such.

She would stand in the center of the stage, facing the audience. She would ask that anyone who desired a demonstration of her abilities to arise. Usually a woman complied with her request. She would address the person somewhat as follows. "You have a problem on your mind. Please concentrate on it. You want to know something about a marriage.

132

You are a widow and are thinking of getting married, but there seems to be an obstacle. Something in the way. You think you have two chances for another marriage, but they are very uncertain chances. One of the men would not marry you on account of your two children. The second man would marry you, but you do not want him. My advice to you is to forget about both of these men. You are thinking about something else. Going into this would necessitate a prediction. As I am not able to foretell events, I must decline taking an answer into consideration. However, I can tell you that you want to know if the person who promised to remember you in his will is going to do so. I am sorry, but as I told you, I am not able to predict." This is a fair sample of what she would tell her subject. Every reading was different. She did not always speak as fast as I have written it. Sometimes she spoke incoherently, or retracted some of the statement she had made. She would continue giving readings until the time allotted to her on the program ran out. She always gave satisfaction.

Mabel was unusually successful in locating stolen or lost articles. One time, at a private reading, a man said his gun had been stolen. He said he was certain he knew who had it, but could not positively identify it, as he did not know the identification number, which consisted of six digits. He knew the first three, and wanted Mabel to tell him the other three. She was able to do this; they were "888." The man recovered his gun. During the night, a small slot machine had been stolen from a small country restaurant, and there was no clue for the detection of the thief. No one had any idea who it might have been or where the machine had been taken. The owner asked Mabel. She told him it had been broken open and the money taken, and that the machine had been abandoned in a wooded tract of land near a river. All such areas were searched, and the missing property was found.

A man once approached Mabel and offered her ten dollars for a reading. His request was refused. He then offered twenty–five dollars; this offer was also refused. He advanced his offer to fifty dollars. On again being refused, he said he would pay any reasonable price she asked. She did not wish to give a reading at any price, but she knew what he wanted, so she told him, 'You are a married man who is interested in another woman, and you want to know something about her. I cannot tell you anything." She received several letters from him begging for a reading, which he never received. I have often thought that if she would have accepted money for her work, she could have become wealthy.

She was never able to explain just how she was able to do such remarkable things. She said she tried to make her mind a blank and especially not to think about things in the immediate vicinity. Some thoughts were bound to come to her. Those thoughts she revealed by speech, and usually they were correct, or sufficiently informative to be of value to the questioner. After having given a public exhibition, Mabel was always deluged with requests for private readings by persons who were willing to pay for them. These requests were nearly always refused, as she never accepted money at any time. All of this had nothing to do with spirit communication, but it was a hard matter to make the "faithful" believe that it didn't.

CHAPTER EIGHT

OTHER SMALL SHOWS, SCHEMES AND FAKES

Small shows of merit playing in small places and con-
ducting their activities on a business basis could always have
money enough to pay expenses and keep moving. Some,
however, would have a show that was not worth the time
spent in reading their advertisements. Some had too many
performers on their salary list and could not take in enough
money to pay them. Some were below par artistically and way
below that in regard to deportment, meaning too much alcohol
and gambling. All shows, big or little, need working capital.
Business was not uniform; sometimes it was a losing proposition for weeks at a time, and money was required to tide the
business over until a spurt of good business would come along
to make up for the losses and bring in a profit besides. I once
had a stretch of three months of poor business, but when it
changed for the better I did not have a poor crowd for two
years.

There were many poor shows playing the small towns.
Only about ten percent of them survived from September to
May, the generally accepted length of the winter theatrical
season. Most of them lasted only a short time before they
found themselves without funds to move on. To recoup their
finances they would seek work in the town, with the women
working in the hotel and the men doing whatever they could
find to do, until they earned enough money to pay transportation home. Sometimes the folks at home sent money, sometimes the show people were so undesirable that the town
people would contribute enough money to enable them to
move on. The lack of business was the fault of the show folk,

usually, and not the town people. When such shows did not draw a crowd, the showmen wrote their poisonous opinion of the town and its inhabitants on the walls and scenery of the "oprey house." The remarks were not complimentary and were sometimes illustrated by crude pictures.

There were some very poor excuses for shows going around the country. The equipment of one old man consisted of a couple of battered suitcases. In one of them he had some badly worn clothes, and in the other, a few inferior magic tricks which he used to give the show. He walked from place to place and begged his meals. Another, more pretentious-looking personage wore an old silk hat. His show consisted of impersonations and imitations. If he was trying to impersonate a dirty old man, he was highly successful. He advertised his show by chalking notices on the sidewalks. He referred to them as "chalk talks."

The worst exponent of our beloved art of magic was a man who styled himself "Professor _____." He was unkempt, slovenly, and dirty. His advertising consisted of one small, printed hand bill, which he carried about the streets, stopping people and holding it for them to read. The bill proclaimed the Professor to be a magician, mimic, and humorist. I happened to be in the town where he was showing and went into the small hall to visit him. His whole outfit was carried in two empty suitcases. Instead of the usual fancy side tables or stands used by magicians, he put an empty soap box on a chair and threw a piece of soiled flowered calico over it, thus giving it some semblance of a table. He made candy, which he sold to his customers. It was a cold compound of powdered sugar, powdered cocoa and canned milk, and when mixed, these ingredients made a pasty mess which he cut into cubes and wrapped in wax paper. The candy may have tasted good, but his hands were dirty and I could not eat the sample he gave me. I heard that his show was worthless.

There was a character known to the natives by the name of Tom. His show consisted of some ancient silent motion pictures. He gave his outdoor show free and depended on the sale of popped corn and peanuts to pay his expenses. He would show half of the picture and then offer the peanuts and popped corn for sale. If sales were not sufficiently large to suit him, he would not finish the picture.

The owner of one small show played a dirty trick on his patrons. He sold a very inferior liniment composed of equal parts of kerosene and vinegar. These ingredients would not mix, so the label read, "Shake Well Before Using." Thousands of bottles of this mixture were sold by this man at fifty cents a bottle in connection with his show. The bottle was not in a paper carton but was wrapped in a common sheet of paper. He would sell the liniment all week. On the last night the bottles were all empty. The sales were always big on this night, and all customers carried home empty bottles. As the mixture was cheap, it would have cost him only a few cents to have had the bottles filled. As soon as the show was over, the grafter and his wife would leave town by way of horse and buggy, driving all night to get away from what might have been an infuriated mob when the deception was discovered.

The selling of his show was a specialty of one so-called magician. He had his local tinner make a lot of cheap magical apparatus. He travelled around, giving shows. At every performance he would announce that he had been giving magic shows for years and had saved an amount of money which would enable him to retire. So, he wanted to sell his magic show. He did this many times, and there always was a bunch of tin can magic equipment ready to be delivered by his hometown tinsmith.

The most glorious and glamorous of all small shows was the medicine show. For about thirty years these shows toured the rural districts, playing in small towns that seldom had any other kind of entertainment. Some towns had Chautauquas during the summer season, but these did not have a blackface song and dance man, and therefore were not acceptable to the majority of the rural people. When a medicine show was advertised, there was as much excitement among the residents of the village as there would be among the small boys in a big city when the circus was coming. They always stayed a week or two, or until they had all the loose change lying around. They gave a number of free shows, and of course, everyone would attend. They gave a different show every night. Twice a week they charged a very small admission, but they kept their best attraction for those nights. On the pay nights, the crowds would always be larger than on the free nights. These companies always had good performers and gave excellent entertainments. These consisted of a number of vaudeville acts, ending with a comedy sketch. Besides doing their own act, all performers worked in the final sketch. These were called "nigger acts" by the performers because the principal character in them was the black face comedian, who was always the hit of the show. Other acts were a ballad singer, a magician, novelty musical numbers, an acrobat, etc. The shows were planned to entertain the country folk.

This type of show was a boon to aspiring performers. Anyone who could do a fairly good act could secure an engagement with a medicine show. The weekly pay was fairly small but certain. Sunday morning was pay time, and the amount paid was always more than enough to cover hotel and laundry expenses. There were advantages for the would-be vaudevillian. First, it was a good place to practice and to get experience. As a performer had to change his act nightly for a week or two, he soon had a big variety of specialties. Besides his own line of work, he also had to take part in comedy acts and short dramas. Of course, he had no opportunity for establishing a reputation for himself, but he could attain enough proficiency in his work to obtain an engagement with a better class of show. Country audiences were always appreciative and gave one confidence in oneself. Many noted performers got their start with a medicine show.

The manager of the show usually owned it and generally was the lecturer who extolled the virtues of the remedies. He always operated under false representations. His pretense was that he was the manager of the show and not the owner. The owner, he said, was a large medicine manufacturer

located in some city. He said this firm was responsible for and
would pay all bills contracted by him, the manager. He said
all the performers were working for a guaranteed salary.
What he was trying to do was to impress on his hearers the fact
that they were a financially sound organization. This was all
deceptive talk, as there was no financial backing, and also no
medicine factory, as all the medicine was made by the show
members behind the scenes in the theatre where no outsiders
were allowed.

The medicines were made in the cheapest way, using the
cheapest drugs it was possible to obtain. The amount received
for the finished product was nearly all profit. Their leading
item was a tonic or blood purifier. I believe there is no such
thing as a blood purifier, but that was the way they designated
it. It consisted of a brown powder made of ground herbs which
had laxative properties. It was packaged in a cheap cardboard
carton appropriately printed with the name and directions for
using it. The directions told the user to place the contents of
the package in one quart of water and allow it to stand for
twenty–four hours, making a quart of liquid medicine which
would last a month and would cure anything that ailed him.
It cost about five cents a package to produce and sold for one
dollar. As most people had some ailment, or thought they did,
thousands of packages were sold. A liniment for aches and
pains was another prominent item. The base of this remedy
was common gasoline, with a few drops of oil of mustard and
red coloring matter to give it a red-hot look. Gasoline cost ten
cents a gallon in those good old days. The irritating qualities
of the mustard gave the impression of heat and, as heat is
associated with the allaying of pain, the user thought he was
heating the place where the liniment was applied. Usually
this thought was sufficient to ease the pain. The biggest cost
of the liniment was the bottle, which was about four cents.
The marked price on the label was fifty cents, but it was sold
at a special advertising price of twenty–five cents. About the
greatest deception and fraud was the healing salve, consisting
mostly of a tin ointment box filled with petroleum jelly. It was

not medicated and its healing qualities were almost nil. It was highly advertised as a cure for itch, eczema, piles, etc. It was priced at twenty-five cents a box and was produced at a cost of about two cents. The corn cure consisted of axle grease in a one ounce ointment box. The cost was about one cent and the sale price was twenty-five cents. These were the principal items sold. Sometimes they had other remedies, like cough cure, catarrh balm, and pep pills,. All of the remedies had one advantage in common, which is that they did not cost much.

These medicines were advertised and sold at night between acts of the show. It required the services of a lecturer to do this. This man was usually called "Doc." He sometimes posed as a doctor. He did not have to be an educated man. His principal requirements were a bold front, a loud voice, unbounded nerve, and a total disregard for the truth. There were such people in those days. He needed no knowledge of medicine. His business was to extol the virtues of the remedies and sell them. At that time there were no laws to regulate the claims which could or could not be made regarding the medicine. The sham doctor could lie about them as much as he desired. He could also guarantee a cure, which is something that cannot be legally done at the present time. The unsophisticated country people believed every word he said and considered him to be a very superior person. Just give one of those lecturers (referred to by the fraternity as "speilers") about fifteen minutes of time for his harangue and he would be able to make everyone in the audience think that he was sick or ought to be, and that the blood purifier would cure anything he might have or be going to have. This same line of talk would be reaching radio and television audiences today if legislation did not forbid it.

At the end of his "speil," the performers would pass among the audience and offer the remedies for sale. Sales were never good at the beginning of the engagement but were always big at the finish. Country people liked to give testimonies for the remedies. One man said that the liniment was helping his rheumatism, but he did not like it because it was sticky. He had been rubbing cough syrup on his leg. Another man came with an empty medicine bottle and wanted some more like it because it had been helping his digestion. He had been taking his wife's female tonic. Some people stood up in the audience and praised the remedies just to draw a little attention to themselves.

A clever but illegitimate method used by the medicine peddlers to sell the dollar package of herbs was to give a positive guarantee to refund the purchase price if the medicine did not affect a cure. With each package they gave the buyer a bank draft for one dollar. This draft was on a reputable bank. When he had used all the medicine and had not been cured, he could send the draft to the bank and receive one dollar. On the face of it, this seemed to be a legitimate proposition. The speiler, however, failed to call attention to certain conditions on the back of the draft which had to be complied with. One had to send a physician's certificate to the effect that he was still suffering with some disease. He had to prove that he had been suffering with that disease before taking the medicine. He had to take oath before a notary public that his statements were true. To do all this would cost more than the dollar he would receive. None of the drafts were ever cashed. It was a good scheme to sell medicine.

Medicine companies sold a soap represented as being different from any other soap and of a superior quality. It did not have lye or rancid fat in it like ordinary soap; instead, it was made from a vegetable oil and the extract of the yucca plant. The root of this plant does have saponaceous qualities, but it was not used in the making of this soap. It was the common coconut oil soap sold in grocery stores, attractively packaged to give it a distinctive look. The fraudulent demonstrations and glib talk of the fakir were what made the sales. One supposed proof showed how the soap lather penetrated the skin. He would wet his hands and rub the bar of soap on them. Rubbing the hands would produce a fine lot of lather and continued rubbing would cause the lather to disappear. The talker would explain that it had been absorbed by the skin. This spectacular quality would cure skin diseases which other remedies would not reach. His hands seemed to be smooth and clean. To prove that the soap had gone back into the skin, he would bring it out. Wetting his hands again and rubbing them caused the lather to appear, which he said was because the soap brought out all the disease and impurities from the skin. That which he said happened, did not happen. The human skin will not absorb anything. What did happen was this: as he rubbed his hands, the water in the lather evaporated. This left the soap forming a thin, invisible coating on the surface of the skin. Only a close inspection would reveal this, and the audience was not invited to make a close inspection. Wetting the hands caused the soap and water to re-form the lather. After this demonstration there was always a good soap sale.

Another tricked test was given to prove the superior lathering qualities of the soap. A large carriage sponge would be offered for inspection. This seemed to be without preparation. The sponge was wetted, and a bar of the soap lightly rubbed into it. Instantly, lather would appear, which would be removed and dropped onto the stage floor. A little more water and squeezing, and more lather would appear. This was also removed and placed on the floor. This was continued until there was a pile of lather on the floor several feet in height, and all from one light rubbing of soap. The secret of this trick was that the sponge was loaded. A bar of soap was dissolved in water. This made a liquid soap with which the sponge was saturated. When the sponge was dry there was no sign of preparation, but there was a whole bar of soap in it to make the high pile of soap on the stage floor. The soap which sold in the grocery store at five cents a bar was sold by the medicine show at the advertising price of two bars for twenty–five cents, and they sold more in a week than a grocer would sell in a year.

The lecturer had many deceptive ways of proving the supposed value of his products. One way was to show how the liniment would improve a person's sense of hearing. Securing a person from the audience who was hard of hearing, he would hold a watch at a distance from him at which he could barely hear it tick; say, two inches. After treating the ear with liniment, the man could hear it tick at a distance of a foot or more. Fine demonstration, wasn't it? But it was a deception. The lecturer had two watches, one with a soft tick, the other with a loud tick, and he manipulated them to suit his purpose.

Another swindle was a method of showing the penetrative qualities of the liniment. The lecturer would exhibit a heavy piece of sole leather. On this, he would pour some liniment. In a few seconds he would show the other side of the leather to be dampened with the liniment. It had gone through the leather. His argument was that if it would penetrate tough leather, it would easily penetrate human tissue and ease pain. The piece of leather used had been prepared for the demonstration; it had been pierced many times with a needle. The holes were not visible, but they made the leather porous and allowed the gasoline liniment to soak through. Many such fraudulent advertisements are being perpetrated on television viewers today, some of them borrowed from the medicine shows of the 1880s and '90s.

Besides fraudulent demonstrations, the lecturers would make many untrue statements. Here is what one Doc said: "If you have a headache, take one teaspoon of the liniment in half a glass of water." "How could a medicine taken into the stomach affect the head?" one of the rustics might ask. "You all know there are two tubes leading from the stomach to the brain. The vapors from the liniment pass up through these tubes to the brain, and their soothing effect stops the pain," was the answer even though the "Doc" had no knowledge of anatomy and frequently used the word "abdum" for abdomen. Another good method of proving that the liniment deadened pain was a fire test. The operator, after rubbing gasoline liniment on his fingers, would hold them in the flame of a candle, with no apparent pain. Again, this was not exactly what it seemed to be. The demonstrator would spread his fingers and pass them through the flame. The flame of burning paraffin was not a very hot one, and his fingers were in it one at a time but not long enough to burn them. As soon as the first finger felt the heat, he would move the second finger into the flame, then the third, and then the fourth. By this time the first finger would be cool, and he could start over again. On one occasion, the trick backfired. The performer applied the liniment to his fingers, but he neglected to allow the gasoline to become dry before he put them in the flame. The gasoline caught fire and severely burned his fingers, and the liniment would not stop that pain.

Another experiment was that of sticking a hatpin through the fleshy part of the arm. After rubbing some liniment on the forearm of an assistant, he would borrow a hatpin from a lady in the audience (they wore them then) and, pulling up a section of the skin and flesh, he would pierce it with the hatpin, which entered at one side and came out at the other. The assistant gave no sign of experiencing pain and walked smilingly through the aisles, exhibiting the punctured arm. The explanation of this trick was that the assistant did experience a little pain, but when the pin reaches the flesh, there is no additional pain. When the pin emerges on the opposite side, there is a slight pain for a moment. The whole performance was no more painful than the insertion of a hypodermic needle into or under the skin. This demonstration sold thousands of bottles of inferior liniment. The greatest mystery of it all to me was why a greasy hatpin out of a woman's hair did not infect the assistant's arm.

A more sensational exhibition was given by a man who allowed his hand to be nailed to a block of wood. That is just what he did, after medicating his hand with the liniment. He placed his palm flat on a large block of wood and allowed a nail to be driven in from the back, through the hand, and into the wooden block. There was a slight amount of bleeding but no evidence of pain. The man went through the audience exhibiting the gruesome sight. The secret was simple, but the act was not easy to do. The nail was not the common carpenter's nail. It was made of silver and was very slender and sharp, like a thick darning needle. The head of the needle was large and of iron, to give the impression that it was a large nail. The man suffered some pain but not as much as might be supposed. The very sharp and smooth body of the nail did not lacerate the skin and other tissue as much as a common nail would. From long practice, he had become somewhat inured to the pain, as he was amply rewarded by large liniment sales. After he had done the trick, he could not use the hand for the same purpose until the wound had healed, which took about three weeks. But he could punish the other hand and have another large liniment sale.

Perhaps the most colossal fraud of all was the curing of a man who was bedridden with rheumatism, causing him to walk and throw away his crutches. Sometimes this would be done after a council of physicians had pronounced him incurable. The supposed cure was made at the theater, but a lot of preliminary work was necessary. First, a suitable patient had to be located. This was done by inquiry. Next, the manager of the medicine show would pay this person a visit. As the sufferer was not able to come to the show, the friendly manager had to visit him and to present him with a free supply of the liniment. He would explain that they were always anxious to treat people with severe cases of rheumatism because when they were able to cure such a case, it would be a big advertisement, and that was why the medicine company came to town. The manager would explain that a case as severe as his would require some time to cure, but as the show would be in town for some time, they would look after him and keep him supplied with liniment without charge. This, of course, pleased the patient and put him in a receptive mood for what was to follow.

After a visit or two, the manager would tell of the last great cure they had made, and how the medicine company had been so grateful for the great advertising they received that the company had presented the cured patient with a check for $1,000. For another, they had paid off the mortgage on his home. For still another, they had paid for a trip to Europe. All this talk would impress the patient, and the idea would enter into his mind that he, too, might receive one of those presents. So, he would commence to speak of his condition as improving, saying the pains were becoming less. He was now ready to be told about the rest of the treatment. He would have to come to the theater on the last night of the show for a final rubbing. In the meantime, he would keep applying the liniment at home. It might be mentioned that the liniment furnished for home use was of better quality than the gasoline and mustard compound sold at the show, as they were fearful that the patient might use too much of the gasoline compound and set the bed on fire. Also, the better quality liniment usually did give some relief.

During the afternoon of the last day of the show's stay the patient would be given a final home rubbing and be told not to exert himself in any way. If he moved at all, it was to be a very slow movement. A conveyance would be sent to take him to the opera house. This would be timed to have him arrive at the show house just before the show started, when the house was filled to capacity. He would walk very slowly (as per instructions) down the center aisle, with the aid of crutches and support on each side. He would be seated on the stage during the show. When the time came for the liniment demonstration, he would walk, still very slowly, to a dressing room, where he would be given another good rubbing with a special liniment. Then he was told to walk as straight and fast as he could out on the stage, carrying the crutches with him. He would do this, the memory of the big presents spurring him to make a special effort.

The sight of the man who an hour before could hardly walk with crutches, walking almost perfectly, was excitingly impressive. The lecturer would break the crutches in two by jumping on them, shouting that the man would never have use for them again. The rheumatic patient would be given assistance in getting home, and the show would leave town the next morning, or if they stayed longer, the patient was told to remain in bed until the liniment affected a completed cure.

Of course this never happened, but the medicine people sold thousands of dollars worth of medicine on the strength of the supposed cure. Also, the rheumatic patient is still waiting for his present.

The local doctors did not approve of the medicine shows and made it their business to oppose them in every way they could. Medicine could be purchased at the theater during the day. Some people did not want to be seen buying medicine and would take advantage of the daytime opportunity. Most of these persons were in debt to the local doctor and did not care to have him know that they were buying from the show. One doctor used his spare time sitting on the curbstone in front of the theater, which kept some of the customers away. Another doctor put a notice in the local newspaper which read, "You can buy your medicine wherever you want to, but before you spend money with anyone else, wouldn't it be a good idea to pay what you owe to the doctor who kept your old carcass out of the grave these many years?"

The medicine show had plenty of other opposition besides the doctors. The druggist thought it was taking money which he should be getting. The minister did not like the idea of people deserting the church prayer meeting night or of their spending money to see shows when it might well find a resting place on the collection plate at Sunday morning church service. The weekly country paper liked to ridicule the medicine show, although this could easily be discouraged by the liberal purchase of advertising space. One newspaper published this squib: "The river has been unusually low this spring, despite the fact that there has been an unusual amount of rain. We finally discovered why. There is a party of fake doctors selling medicine at the opera house." No amount of opposition from the minority of the self-appointed upper class of the town had any effect, however, on the business done by the medicine peddlers. The common majority was always with them, supporting them and spending with them all the money they could afford, and in many instances, money they could not afford. When it was all said and done, the medicine show made money, and that was their real reason for coming to town.

Another lever for prying money out of medicine show patrons was the Popular Lady Contest. Ostensibly this was a voting contest to determine which lady of the town could receive the most votes, which would give her the distinction of being the most popular lady and the winner of the diamond ring. In reality it was a scheme to get friends of the candidates to spend money to win the election. This idea was not a new one, as it has been used for many years in governmental elections. Votes were given free (?) with medicine sales, one vote given with each cent spent. This meant that whoever could purchase the most medicine would have the most votes to cast and could control the election. Candidates for the election were supposedly chosen by a primary election, but as the show manager handled and counted all the votes, he could put up any candidate he wished to, and that was just what he did. He would arrange it so there would be girls on the list with followings that might be antagonistic towards each other. For instance, in a long list of candidates there would be names of girls whose fathers, brothers, or beaus were of different religious opinions, or who differed in politics, or who were business rivals, or who were just plain enemies. The voting was continued from night to night, and the standing of the contestants was printed on a large bulletin board placed where it could be viewed by the audience. Toward the end of two weeks of voting, excitement over the contest ran very high. Opposing factions would buy more and more medicine to obtain votes to boost their favorite lady.

As the showman did all the vote counting, he would arrange the score to keep the contestants at a fairly even level. By the time the last night arrived, some of the electioneers were ready to, and did, spend large sums of money in order to win the contest. Sometimes they engaged in a fist fight over the matter. One man worked against his niece so hard that he incurred the enmity of the whole village to such an extent that he was ostracized. His neighbors would not talk to him. He became so despondent that he committed suicide. Husband and wife took opposite sides in a contest and fought so bitterly against each other that it led to a divorce. In one town the show ran out of medicine and a contestant offered to buy the show if she could get votes with it. In one place they counterfeited the votes. In another place someone broke into the opera house and stole a lot of votes. All this to win a cheap, chip diamond ring. For a number of years these contests were conducted by small and large shows throughout the nation. In most states they were finally abolished by law.

Many small shows had methods of obtaining money other than by admission. The manager of one show conducted it as a cover up for crooked gambling. He was adept at cheating at games of cards. His show would take him to small towns, where he could win anytime he wanted to. After showing in a town for a week, he had all the loose money there was around. The wife of the owner of another show canvassed the town selling gasoline heated flat irons and hand operated vacuum cleaners. This was in the days before electricity was available in rural communities. This woman frequently made a larger profit than the show did.

A man and his wife, who had little entertaining ability, tried to run a show but frequently found themselves on the rocks. They had still another method for raising funds. For just such emergencies they carried with them a quantity of printed labels and ingredients for making a cheap medicine. When they experienced financial difficulties, they would quit showing and establish themselves in the medicine business. They would borrow a metal washtub, which they would fill with the principal ingredient of the medicine, water. They medicated the water with powdered licorice, aloes, and morphine. Anyone could buy morphine in those days. They would buy some bottles from the local druggist, which they would fill with the medicine. The total cost of the bottle of medicine, which according to the label cured everything, was about six cents. There was enough morphine in each dose to stop any ache or pain for a while. With a horse and buggy from the livery stable, they would drive through the country peddling the remedy to the credulous farmers, who would sometimes buy it in large quantities at one dollar a bottle. When the couple could not purchase bottles from the druggist, they would search the alleys and dumps and collect any old bottles they could find, wash them, and use them for their medicine. When sales were slow, they would reduce the price to three bottles for a dollar and still make a profit. In a few weeks, they would have enough money to re-establish themselves in the show business and begin another cycle. A novel method was used by two married couples who found themselves stranded when their show closed without notice. Being in a strange community and penniless was a humiliating situation, but these people were equal to the occasion. They begged someone with a horse and wagon to haul them and their baggage to a nearby town where they were not known. Here, they would secure rooms and board at any place someone would take them in. They would represent themselves as being in the organ repair business. They would rent any old building or shed to use as a shop. They paid no board or rent money in advance. They could not, because they were broke. They would canvass the town, soliciting organ repair work. At that time many homes had an organ and most of them needed repair. As soon as there were four organs in the shop the repair work would commence. Of course, material and parts for the organs were needed, and those were things the stranded showmen did not have; neither did they have the money to buy them. They overcame this difficulty easily. They would take unworn and usable parts from three of the organs and use them to repair the fourth. When this organ was delivered and paid for, they would use the money to purchase repairs for the other three organs. When these were delivered and paid for, they would use the money to pay their board, and bills. After a month or so, they would have enough money to get back in the show business and give it another try. I never found out just what they would have done if they had not been able to secure any organs to repair.

The most despicable scheme was the one used by a showman in the days when tin tags were given with plugs of chewing tobacco. This was a commodity which seemed to be necessary for some people's existence at that time. These tags could be exchanged for merchandise of all kinds, which had values ranging from as low as 25 cents for a cheap fountain pen requiring 100 tags, up to an upright piano, which could be purchased for 250,000 tags. This showman would announce to his audience that in his hometown there was a young woman who was partially paralyzed and confined to a wheel-chair. She was an accomplished pianist, and if she had a piano, she could support herself by giving piano lessons. He said there was a drive on at home to collect enough tags to secure a piano for her. As she required a large number of tags, he was soliciting them from members of his audience. The unsuspecting country folk contributed generously by collect-ing all the tags they could and giving them to the showman. The truth of the matter was that there was no paralyzed young woman, and the showman did not have a hometown. The cheap crook used the tags to exchange for fishing tackle, a rifle, and other, similar goods.

An enterprising man and wife who travelled with a show had a clever system for making a little change. At every hotel in which they stopped, they would examine the upholstered furniture to find anything of value which might have slipped between the cushion and the body or arm of the chair. They could usually find small articles like a comb, scissors, and pencil. Occasionally they found money. They pursued this little racket for years. They would be given a hotel room, and as soon as it had been searched, they would find some fault with it and ask for another one. When being shown rooms, they would try to get the clerk to leave for a moment, so they could make a quick search of the room. They would look over several rooms in this manner, and the husband would engage the clerk in conversation in one room while the wife searched the others.

If the travelling people were crooked in some of their

methods, the simple-minded rural folk were not so dumb themselves, and they had clever methods of their own for obtaining money. One very small village was the birthplace of a noted general of the Indian wars. The remains of his old home were still there, and horse and buggy travellers would stop to inspect it. One of the villagers, more for fun than anything else, told one of the travellers that the pipe he was smoking had been the general's property and that he had found it in the attic of the house. The tourist immediately offered him five dollars for it, which the native accepted. This gave him an idea. He scoured the country and collected all the useless and worn-out pipes he could find. In exchange for them, he gave a new corncob pipe worth a nickel. He made it his business to loaf around the general's birthplace and play the same game on other travellers. He sold many pipes. If there was no pipe sale, he had a one-cent piece on which were scratched the general's initials. He said he'd found in the woodshed. This (or these) also sold readily. When he could not secure pennies of sufficient age, he used some of more recent date. The purchasers never seemed to notice the discrepancy.

In a southern state, a resident of a small community earned some money selling Confederate soldiers caps. He manufactured them and would put one of them in the garret of his home after soiling and mutilating it to give it the appearance of the genuine article. I do not know how much he charged for them, but it was probably whatever he could get. Later, he found out that such caps could be purchased from manufacturers of uniforms, and he obtained his supply from them. In a certain large city there was a furniture factory which made imitation antique furniture. There was no deception about this, as the goods were plainly marked "imitation antique." A clever ruralist would purchase this furniture, remove the label, and store it in his garret, where it would become dusty. He sold the furniture at a good price to unsuspecting travellers. Of course connoisseurs in this line would have detected the deception immediately.

At a place on the shore of one of the Great Lakes there

was the remains of a wooden battleship. Embedded in the wood were a few lead bullets fired by the British. A resident picked out some of these bullets, melted them, and molded the lead into little anchors. for a ready sale to visitors. When the bullet supply was exhausted, the unsophisticated country jake made anchors out of an old lead pipe. These sold as easily as the genuine article.

There is a plant of uncertain identity that grows in the Red Sea area, known as the Rose of Jerico or the Rose of Sharon. It is a common weed in its native country. During the dry season it closes into a ball, but when the rainy season comes along, the plant opens up and turns green. For this reason, it is also called a Resurrection Plant. A similar plant is native to the southwestern United States. They are quite a curiosity and may be obtained from most large dealers in flowers and seeds. Some persons travel and canvas homes, offering them for sale. This is a legitimate procedure. One woman had a scheme for selling them that was not quite legal. She misrepresented the plants. She said they were named the Resurrection Plant because they bloomed only at Easter-time, when a white flower with three petals would grow from the center of the plant. The petals would drop off after three day; she said this was indicative of the three days Christ was in the tomb. She had a photograph to show what the plant looked like when open and in bloom. The plant did not bloom. The photo was tricked, as the white flower was an artificial one placed on the plant when the photo was made. The picture was quite convincing, and many sales were made. The woman told me she had travelled for years selling them, and that she owned a lot of property purchased with money realized from sales of "Resurrection Plants."

While on the subject of frauds, I will relate an incident which occurred in a small town in the midwest. One morning I went into the general store to make some purchases. A showcase contained some curious looking articles, which the storekeeper said were Indian relics that had been dug up in the surrounding country. They did not have the appearance of anything the American Indians might have made; rather, they resembled things that might have come from Egypt. There were small cups, bowls, little crude human figures, something that resembled a candle-stick, little spheres which might be marbles, a group of four cubes with dots on the side like dice, and numerous unidentifiable objects, all made out of clay and baked. There was a box-shaped affair with a loose lid, with a figure of a winged sphinx on the lid. It was thought to be a jewel casket. There was a clay tablet, marked with characters telling of the great Biblical flood. Another marked tablet told of a battle between two tribes. There were short stemmed pipes, the bowls having a shape like a human head and face. No one in the sparsely settled country had any idea where their origin might have been, though some seemed to think they were of modern construction and buried as a hoax, to be discovered and sold to credulous travellers.

There was a Mr. A there who was under suspicion. He could locate the buried articles easier than anyone. Others had difficulty in locating anything at all. For this reason it was thought that he made them and buried them, although no one could offer proof that he did. The articles were all made of clay, and the soil for miles around was pure sand. Mr. A could not travel any distance to procure clay, as he had no horse and buggy to make the journey. If he had been able to procure the clay, he would have had no chance to make the relics, as he lived in a very small house which was open to visitors at all times, as was the custom with country people at that time. There was no privacy. He had a shed beside the house, but this was also open. There was no opportunity to have them shipped in, as the village was a very small one where everyone knew his neighbors' personal affairs. In addition, the articles exhumed were so numerous that no one person could have made them all. Also, small bushes, weeds, and grass grew on the places Mr. A dug into.

The fact remained, however, that Mr. A could always locate the ancient burial places. I induced Mr. A to take me with him on a digging expedition one hot Sunday morning.

We dug for hours with no results. Finally, we decided to quit and that I should go back alone the next morning and do some more digging. I did this and had not dug far when I unearthed two very large articles shaped like Indian arrowheads but made of slate. I was suspicious that Mr. A had planted them there the day before, but there was no evidence to indicate such a fact. Mr. A would have had to walk a long way out into the country if he did place them there; and no one knew where he would have been able to locate slate.

I purchased the jewel casket, the flood tablet, and a pipe from Mr. A. When I got back to more settled country, I showed the relics to students and others who might be competent to give an opinion about them. All were puzzled and were unable to decide on their authenticity, though they leaned to the belief that they were fraudulent. Finally I presented them to a museum of natural history. The scientists there would express no definite opinion. After a few years I read in a newspaper that scientists from the state capitol were being guided by Mr. A and were discovering similar specimens in another and distant part of the state. The news article also mentioned the peculiar fact that no one but Mr. A could locate the burial places.

ANNUAL TOUR OF

RAPP

THE MAGICIAN

INTRODUCING THE FOLLOWING NOVELTIES

ORIENTAL BLACK ART

A Midnight Mystery as Practiced by the Yogis of India.

People, tables, chairs and other objects appear and disappear before your eyes without being covered for an instant, being one of the most complicated and unexplainable effects ever shown. Everything used in this elaborate production is carried by MR. RAPP, even the scenery and lights.

The Floating
Fairy ❧
In which the body of a Living Lady is suspended in mid-air without any support. Also known as

The Maid of
the Moon
For which Beautiful Costumes have been designed to represent the following:—

THE DANCING GIRL,
STATUE OF JUSTICE,
MORNING, NOON, NIGHT,
SAILOR GIRL, COLUMBIA

The Stove Pipe Mystery

A European Novelty Somewhat Out of the Ordinary.

PUZZLING TO EXTREMES.

156

CHAPTER NINE

MY FINISH

When it is all said, and I think I have said it all, it amounts to the fact that I gave magic shows for nearly sixty continuous years. If any other magician gave shows for a greater length of time, I am not aware of the fact. I do not know whether I was a good magician or not because I could not sit out in the front to watch my show and judge its merits. I must have been good, though, because every good magic show I saw was doing the same tricks I did. One thing that is certain is that if I am not good now, I never will be.

Magic does not have the same standing in the entertainment world that it had when I first became interested in it. At that time, magicians were a scarcity. Magic was cloaked with mystery. The average person knew nothing about its secrets. It was generally supposed that only a few people in the world were competent to be magicians, and that they possessed some occult power. A magician was considered to be a superior being; and magic was an educational and very aristocratic form of entertainment; the kind sponsored by royalty. Today it has degenerated into a leg or girl show. I suppose something had to take the place of the old burlesque shows which featured legs. In the old days, magical apparatus was expensive and exclusive. Today it can be bought in the ten- cent store. Every little boy knows how tricks are done, or thinks he does. There are about 100,000 magicians around now, and most of them are bad. It is said that all magicians are crazy or they would not try to be magicians. I am not prepared to argue on that point, as I am one of them. The present slump in magic is only temporary. Let a generation or two go by and an interest in magic will revive in a new crop of new humans. But by that time, all present day good magicians will be dead, myself among them. For that reason, magicians should specialize in longevity instead of cute, underdressed lady assistants. There are a few sturdy, hard-fighting magicians who are striving to uphold the traditions of magic, but they are having a hard time of it. They are not the kind we meet on the corner, greeting us with, "Did you see this one?" or "Take a card." Things are screwy, but I am still glad I am a magician, although I sometimes think I should have tried to earn a living by honest means, instead of by lies and deception.

It is a long way from 1883, when I gave my first, dinky magic act. Those years were happy and prosperous ones, and I have been financially successful, although not rich. I earned and always had enough money so that I never had to worry about a place to sleep or how I was going to pay for the three or four meals a day which I was accustomed to having. Neither did I have to wonder how I was going to pay for a new suit of clothes or shoes. I have been able to save enough money to take care of myself now that I have retired. At first the going was rather tough. Sometimes I felt like giving up and going back to the dry goods business. I struggled along, never loafing, never having a vacation, and never missing a night's showing until I finally learned to conduct a small town magic show and make money at it. I fought storms, fires, floods, epidemics, heat, cold, and the Depression. Having a good show and keeping everlastingly at it was responsible for my success. In spite of all the misfortunes, I am emphatic in saying that I would be a magician again if I were to relive my life and knew what I know now. I have been able to live in the open in summer, which has helped to keep me physically well; and magic's numerous perplexing problems have kept my brain cells active. There is no mental stagnation for the busy, wide awake magician.

Association with the kind of people I found in the country

(exceptions allowed for), who were genuine, free from sophistication, honest, and frank, is compensation for any disadvantages a small town show might have. I would be at it still, had not the gas shortage in the war compelled me to stop. And now that the war is over — well, I realize I am seventy–five. The years are many. I feel it wisdom not to start out again. Possibly the rural fields of my endeavors are less fertile now. As things are I am very well satisfied with a life which has been a contented one. Contacts with my fellow beings have all been happy ones. No one has ever cheated me out of a cent. I have never been snubbed by anyone. I have always been treated in a most respectful manner. The only person who ever used an oath in speaking to me was, of all things, a woman. I was so humiliated by the affair that I moved out of her house and out of the city. Outside of that, everything has been lovely. My wish is that everyone in the world might be as healthy, happy and contented as I am.

In looking back, I find that some changes have taken place in the city of Milwaukee, where I now live. The old time wash woman is now a laundress, bookkeepers are accountants, undertakers are morticians, doctors' office girls are laboratory technicians, hired girls are maids, but garbage collectors are still garbage collectors. Horses and midwives have disappeared completely from the scene. Old soldiers used to sit around the stove in the rear of small grocery stores, spitting tobacco and re-fighting the Civil War battles. They are gone, but they have been replaced by a group of old pensioners who sit in the park and run the federal government from the iron benches. It's "agin" the law to spit on the sidewalk, so they cuss and swear instead. Well, I am getting old. I believe that I am in my second childhood, because I am commencing to think I would like to have a babysitter. After sixty years of ups and downs (mostly downs), I remember the joy I have brought to many thousands, especially the happiness I brought to children. They all called me Uncle Gus. I was the world's second greatest uncle, Uncle Sam being the first. I have lived from candles to neon and from ox carts to jet planes. Young folk are speeding things up lately, and it is hard for me to keep up with the times. I have weak legs, my eyes are dim, and I have had to provide myself with dentures. Once in a while I am dizzy and see spots. Outside of those few defects, I am all right. It is about time I thought of dying. Why not? It's being done every day by some of our most distinguished citizens. I don't see why I can't be in the swim. I have sufficient funds to pay for a mediocre funeral with a clergyman, flowers and other trimmings. There might even be a free lunch and dance after the burial. I am satisfied with the world as it was and is. I am not worrying about what the world is coming to, as I won't be there enough to find out, although I do worry about where I might be going to. Amen.

EPILOGUE

Shortly after the publication of his book in 1959, Jay and Frances Marshall brought Gus Rapp to see me.

"What do you think of the introduction Bob Parrish wrote for your book?" Jay asked him.

"Oh," said Gus, "I never care what they say about me."

At that time, Gus was living alone in a furnished room in Milwaukee and passing the time by studying Spanish. "I'm at the head of the class," he said, "but that hardly counts as I have nothing else to do." He was a spry, fragile old man with eyes that genuinely twinkled.

That Christmas he sent me a hand–lettered card with the inscription, "My legs are weak, my eyes are dim and I am slightly goofy in the head, but I am still able to extend to you Seasons Greetings."

The following year his health failed. He had a leg removed and was confined to a nursing home, but magicians who looked in on him reported him to be cheerful. Frances Marshall commented that he was a man who never complained except in jest.

Francis Augustine Rapp died July 30, 1961, in his 90th year. A Requiem Mass was sung for him in St. Anthony's Church, Milwaukee, and members of the International Brotherhood of Magicians and the Houdini Club of Wisconsin served as pallbearers.

Robert Parrish

APPENDIX

MY CONTEMPORARIES

ALEXANDER HERRMANN

Alexander Herrmann seems to be the most celebrated magician of all times. He was unlike any other magician as he had a personality strictly his own. Others might have easily copied his tricks, but not his outstanding characteristics. His resemblance to the supposed appearance of Satan was all in his favor. When he smiled, he looked like a loveable devil; and he smiled most of the time. His movements were graceful. He seemed to be walking on an air cushion as he moved about the stage. His general make up was charming. He mixed subtle humor with his talk. He billed himself as the "Necromatique Comedian," but he did not allow his wit to detract from his skill. His show was 100 percent high-class conjuring entertainment. His slight French accent enhanced his versatile personality. He needed no gaudy, half-dressed females to bolster his performance. He used his wife, Adelaide, for illusions and spectacular dances. Dot Robinson was his stage assistant. Of course, there was the inevitable Bumsky, the colored assistant.

Mrs. Herrmann wore expensive formal dresses. Herrmann dressed in court costume; that is, dress coat and vest, knee pants, silk stockings, and slippers with buckles. Dot Robinson wore a neat, black velvet page costume. Herrmann used very little special scenery. His opening act and most of his show was given in a stage set called "Center Door Fancy," which was a drawing room or parlor scene with a large center door. A few illusions required a special setting. He did not have the advantage of our present day controllable electric lights. Gas was the illuminant. The lighted jets could all be extinguished at the same time with the turn of one valve, but when the many jets were to be relighted at one time, it was a problem. This was solved by having a continuous line of jets across the stage in the footlight trench. They were very close to each other, so that when one jet was lighted, its flame would light the jet next to it and so on across the whole stage. It took about five seconds for all of the jets to be lighted. For extra illumination he had calcium lights in the balcony with powerful reflectors throwing their illumination on the stage. Herrmann played in high-class theatres only and charged their highest prices. The gallery, called peanut heaven, was 25 cents and was always crowded. Orchestra seats were $2.50, a high price at that time.

As with any other magician, things sometimes went wrong for the master. At one time, whoever arranged his apparatus was at fault. A nested set of cups used for the hat production had not been placed in its proper place behind the center table. Herrmann was in the habit of reaching for it without looking at it and loading it into the hat. When he reached for it this time it wasn't there, so he had to look and reach again. He also looked off stage at the assistant, made an ugly face, and muttered something. At another time, during the Noah's Ark illusion, a sliding panel opened slightly, allowing a little pig to stick one foot out. He squealed as only a little pig can. Dot Robinson and other assistants looked off stage to give the audience the impression that the squeal came from there. I don't know if this misdirection impressed the audience or not, but it seemed to me that the squeals came from the concealed pig with one leg sticking out. At still another time, he had loaded a coil of paper ribbon inside a boy's blouse and commenced to withdraw it, saying, "I see you had noodles for dinner." Just then, what was left of the unwound coil was pulled out and fell on the floor. Nothing dismayed Herrmann, who picked it up and laughingly said, "I see you also had pancakes."

Herrmann also liked to do tricks in public places for advertising purposes. In Milwaukee he would go to the

German Market, buy a dozen rolls, and, breaking them, find a gold piece in each one. The bewildered woman who sold the rolls would break open every one she had left, but no gold pieces. In a barber shop, the barber would discover that the magician still had a beard after his face had been shaved; at least, so I have been told.

He delighted in entertaining newspapermen. His travelling equipment consisted of three railroad coaches. One was a passenger coach for the people, one carried his stage equipment, and the third carried a tallyho coach and the four horses used to draw the coach. Also, a saddle horse was there for Herrmann's personal use. He would load all the newspaper boys into and on top of the coach and with a bugler to add atmosphere to the affair, would give them a ride about town.

The Herrmanns (there were several of them), all magicians, were gentlemen of a high caliber as well as linguists and scholars. They elevated the status of magic from that of a strolling street corner performer to that of a worthy and honorable profession.

HARRY KELLAR

Kellar was strictly an American magician. He was born in Erie, Pennsylvania and for a long time the house where he was born bore a bronze tablet stating the fact. The house was finally torn down to make room for improvements. Kellar started out by being an assistant to a magician named Hughes, who travelled under the title of "the Fakir of Ava." The youthful Kellar obtained all of his early magical training from this man. At a very early age he took his own show on the road. His experiences were not a path of roses.

When I was a very young man, I had an interview with him. Realizing that I was very enthusiastic about becoming a magician, he said, "Don't build your hopes too high on the amount of money you expect out of magic, because I travelled for fifteen years before I made more than enough to cover living expenses." Most of the time he didn't do as well as that. On several occasions he had to give up the show business and engage in other activities in order to keep from becoming destitute. Sometimes he travelled with other shows. He was the advance agent for Davenport Bros. and Fay, the notorious fraudulent spiritualists of the last century. At one time he joined forces with two Germans and made up a trio who styled themselves the "Royal Illusionists," and they did a Chinese act. On re-opening his own show in the United States, business wasn't too good, but by keeping everlastingly at it, he finally managed to build up a good reputation which resulted in good business for the rest of his career.

Kellar gave a show which was different from all others. His performance was strictly one of mystery. He used little or no comedy, and he always maintained a dignified and conservative manner. He was the personification of a modern sphinx. His best-remembered trick was the growth of two rose bushes in flower pots. The roses grown were real ones, and they were clipped off and presented to ladies in the audience. Nearly all of his tricks differed from those done by other magicians. His principal large illusions were the Simla Seance and Fly To. The Kellar show had an individuality as distinguished as that of Kellar himself. His stage helpers were boys. His wife was the only woman in the show. After about thirty years, he turned the show over to Howard Thurston and retired in comfortable circumstances to live in Los Angeles.

In 1911 Heinrich Keller had his name legally changed to Harry Kellar, the name he had made famous. He was appointed the Dean of the Society of American Magicians after he retired in 1908. Kellar died in Los Angeles, California on March 10, 1922 at the age of seventy–two.

HOUDINI

During my younger days I had many names attached to me. As soon as I was able to recognize a name I was called

Gussie, which now sounds a little bit sissified to me. Later I was called Frankie, then Gus. When I started using Augustus, someone called me August, and others called me Gust, or Gustave. Because I was a decidedly yellow blonde I was dubbed Blondie or Cotton Top. Because I had a long nose they called me "Nosey." Some pepped my ego by addressing me as a professor. I have reason to believe that some called me names I am glad I didn't hear. My old friend Harry Houdini referred to me as Augustavious.

Regarding Houdini I have good reasons for believing that I knew him for a greater length of time than anyone outside of his family, because we played in the city streets when we were little boys. At that time, neither of us knew that there was such a thing as magic; for that matter, neither of us knew that we played together. In after years we reasoned it out this way: in the city where we lived there was a vacant block called the Haymarket. Farmers from the surrounding country would bring in loads of hay, locate in the square, and wait for someone to come along and buy it. This was a fine spot for the neighborhood boys to congregate and do whatever boys can think of doing when they run wild. One day a farmer brought his dog along and chained him to a wagon wheel. For some reason the horses moved forward a bit and the dog became entangled in the wheel, breaking its leg. It had to be shot. As the entire gang of boys played in a bunch and we both remembered seeing the dog accident, we decided that we had played together when we were little boys.

I met Harry in later years when he and another man (not his brother Hardeen) were doing the box trick which was later named "Metamorphosis" and using the name "Houdini Bros." Harry was a busy man, but he always had time for a visit with me when I called on him. On one occasion I phoned him and said I wanted to make an appointment to call on him. He said, "You don't have to get permission to call on me. Come anytime you want to." I said, "I want to pick out a time when you aren't busy." He laughed and answered, "If you want to wait for such a time you are out of luck, because there is no such time."

Harry was a notoriously bad dresser. At one time I waited at the stage door for him to arrive for the matinee. It was a high-class vaudeville house in a big city. From time to time other acts on the bill entered. They all had the appearance of being millionaires, as they were well-dressed in the height of fashion. When Houdini, the star, came along, I almost mistook him for a janitor or fireman reporting for duty. Bessie had on a hat which I had seen her wear in a motion picture taken three years earlier. Harry explained his lack of attention to his personal appearance by saying that he did it to please his mother. The Weiss family was a poor one and not accustomed to good clothes, and when Harry's mother saw him in good clothes, he seemed like a stranger. So to please his mother he always wore old clothes. Harry was strictly a mother's boy.

I received a letter which mentioned Harry from a friend of mine who was a vaudeville performer. He said, "I worked the Standard Club last week for the head of the Orpheum Circuit, Mort Singer, and he brought Houdini the handcuff man. He was playing at the State Lake and came down between shows to do a magic act for the kids. He went on ahead of me so I was able to watch his act. Of all the punk magic acts for kids, he had it. It reminded me of the bum magic acts I used to do. In fact, I believe I was better. Here is his routine: Tape around neck; Wine and Water (piece of black silk); kerchief, eggs, fire (in double container); rabbit (got this muddled); tying a kerchief in knots (knots gone); pack of needles, thread, etc.; and Sucker Box (did it rotten). You would have laughed your head off if you had seen all of this; and by the way, Houdini is a nifty dresser. My suit is three years old and his was worse than mine. Well, anyway, he was a good movie actor, as you will remember, so I will quit roasting your old friend. It all shows that those fellows are not so good as us little guys when they get away from their fine audiences in comfortable seats in a beautiful theatre with good lights and big orchestra to back them up."

While the general public regarded Houdini as the greatest magician of all times, he was not considered to be such by professional showmen. They considered him a great showman but not a great magician. Houdini understood this situation as well as anyone. One time during a visit I remarked that I was thinking of making up a magic act to play vaudeville. He said, "If you do, I can get you two year's booking on big time in Europe." I said that I thought the act would not be good enough for big time. He said, "You'd be surprised at what poor acts are playing big time. Take me for instance. You can't say that I do anything good. That needle threading trick has been done by every street corner side show and fairground magician for the last hundred years. That water tank illusion is sensational, but it isn't anything that could be called good. My value lies in the drawing power of my name. My name in front of a theatre will fill the house, no matter how poor my stage show is." That is what Houdini thought of the Great Houdini.

HOWARD THURSTON

Howard Thurston was another friend of long standing. When I first met him, his whole outfit consisted of some decks of playing cards, a string of baby clothes, a live goose, and a very young colored boy named George White. Howard was still new in the magic business then, and neither of us knew that one day he would head the world's largest magic show. He had been giving shows in small towns in the South, playing mostly to Negroes and at the time we first met he had decided to go after the white patronage. As I had been showing in small towns, he pumped me for all the information he could get. At that time, the back hand card palm (erroneously so called) was brand new, and he imparted its secret to me. He said he had learned it from a Cuban. In return, I told him about some of the tricks I was using, which were new to him. This was about 1898, and our friendship continued until his death in 1936. In the late twenties Howard Thurston and Doc

Finkle tried to get me to join the International Brotherhood of Magicians and even signed an application blank vouching for me. It was almost twenty years later when I did join the I.B.M., and a new application with a new price (higher) was filled out for me. I have kept the old blank signed by Thurston and Doc Finkle.

BLACKSTONE HOME

For many years Harry Blackstone made his home in Colon, Michigan, on an island in a lake about half a mile from the village. Here is where he spent his summers and here is where his son Harry recieved his education. When at home, the older Harry was one of the villagers and young Harry played in the town band. The island, which covered a number of acres, was a beautiful and well-kept spot; and it had a large number of fine shade trees. Part of it was a farm operated by "Farmer Blackstone," who grew mint. Harry had a unique collection of old street lighting lampposts, and these odd articles were to be found on all parts of the island. When the show closed in the spring, he would come to Colon, with the show equipment and about a dozen of his glamour girls, whom he would board during the summer. Some of the girls were out of Colon families and today, many of them are living in the village as middle-aged women.

Sally Banks was general manager of the island and a superintendent of the household. Sally and her husband had travelled with the show until Mr. Banks died, when Sally took charge of the island. During the winter she lived alone in the house, which was not a very agreeable occupation on a deserted island surrounded by ice. During a blizzard she would be cut off from civilization (meaning Colon) for three days to a week. There would be plenty of food and fuel, but what would she do if she were to become ill, her friends would ask her. Sally didn't know, but the question set her to thinking, and she devised a scheme. The house was visible across the lake to a lot of Colon people. She told her friends that if she needed help at any time, she would place a red light bulb in the window. Anyone seeing this would know that Sally was in trouble and would go to her aid. At Christmas time she thought she was entitled to a tree, and so she obtained one, decorated it, and placed it near the window. It so happened that the only red bulb on the tree was on the side near the window. When she illuminated the tree she turned on the warning light, and in a short time a large share of Colon's population was at her door to find out what was wrong. There was nothing wrong with Sally. There never was.

SIX NIGHT PROGRAM

Monday
Small Tricks: Rising Cards
                                 Talking Skull
                                 Hat-Watch-Tumbler
                                  and Handkerchief
                                 Flower Cornucopia
                                 Egg Bag and Rooster
Sale
Musical Glasses (one person)
Shorty Show
Announcements
Comedy Sketch

Tuesday
Small Tricks: Watch Manipulating
                                 Rice Bowls-Devil Sticks
                                 Card Slate (torn corner)
                                 Wine and Water Changes
                                 Nest of Boxes
Sale
Ventriloquism
Substitution
Rag Pictures
Announcements
Comedy Sketch

Wednesday
Small Tricks: Card Manipulating
                                 Diminishing Deck
                                 Thumb Tie
                                 Cake in Hat
                                 Silk Production (Flag)
Sale
Punch and Judy
Chapeaugraphy
Mabel—Mental Act
Marionettes
Announcements

Comedy Sketch
Thursday
Small Tricks: Thimble Manipulating
                                       Four Aces
                                       Cut and Restored Rope
                                       Little Egg Bag (Malini)
                                       Torn and Restored Napkin
                                       Sun and Moon

Sale
Spirit Cabinet
Finger Shadows
Comedy Skit
Illustrated Songs
Serpentine Dance
Friday
Small Tricks: Bills and Balls
                                        Handkerchief and Lemon
                                       Aerial Treasury
                                       Counting Money (Money Tray)
                                       Inexhaustible Hat
                                       Birth of the American Flag

Sale
Musical Act: Glasses (four hands)
                                       Bottles
                                       Bowls
                                       Sleigh Bells

Aerial Suspension
Comedy Sketch
Saturday
Small Tricks: Exposing Magic
                                       Linking Rings
                                       Trouble Wit

Sale
Shorty Show
Musical Act: Cow bells
                                       Xylophone
                                       Musical Funnels

Comedy Sketch

COMEDY SKETCH

"Photograph Gallery"

Characters: Straightman (S)
              Comedian (C)
Setting: Old room with remains of old camera with head
        cover. Chair for sitter. Rude picture of face
        on one side of a large piece of cardboard, with
        donkey on other side.

Enter Straightman.
S: I find myself in a strange town and dead broke, not a cent
of money in my pocket and no money to buy food with. I rented
this old room to sleep in. This used to be a photograph gallery,
and I find here the remains of an old camera, not even a lens
in it. I put a sign at the foot of the stairs reading "Photograph
Gallery"; now, if I could get hold of some half-baked person I
could pretend to take his picture, get my pay in advance, and
then I could leave town.
Knock, and Comedian enters.
S: Come in.
C: I am in.
S: Well, now that you are in, what do you want?
C: I want to get took.
S: Well, I don't want you.
C: You can't have me. I want to get took.
S: Oh, you want me to take your picture.
C: No, you can't take my picture, 'cause I ain't got none
    yet.
S: You want me to make a picture that looks like you.
C: That's what I want, I want to get took.
S: I know what you mean; first, I'll make you acquainted
    with my prices.
C: No, I don't want to get acquainted with no one.
    I just want to get took.

S: I mean that I'll tell you how much it will cost.

C: Oh! Does it cost something to get took?

S: Sure it does—and I always get my fees in advance.

C: (Excitedly) No you don't! You don't get fleas in my pants!

S: I mean, I get my pay before I make the picture. Now, the first dozen will cost you five dollars. The second dozen will cost you two dollars; and the third dozen, you get free of charge.

C: Fine. I'll take the third dozen first.

S: No you won't. You'll take the first dozen first. Now, what style of picture do you want?

C: Sure, I want a stylish picture.

S: I mean, what kind do you want? Do you want a bust picture?

C: No, I don't want no busted picture. I want a good one.

S: I mean, do you want to be taken from here up?

C: Now, wouldn't I look nice, running around from here down.

S: I mean, do you want to be taken in half?

C: Gosh no, I don't want to be cut in half!

S: Well, what kind of a picture do you want?

C: I want to be taken in a group.

S: You'll have to have more people to sit with you, if you want to be taken in a group.

C: (To audience) All right, some of you fellows, come sit with me.

S: For every extra person in the group, it will cost you a dollar a dozen extra.

C: Never mind, fellows—stay where you are.

S: Now, let's get down to business. First, I will make a negative of you.

C: No, you don't. I don't want to be taken naked

S: I mean that I will expose you.

C: That's just as bad as being taken naked.

S: I mean, I will put your face on a plate.

C: No, you don't. If you put my face on a plate, some of those fellows out there will think it is free lunch and eat it.

S: Now let's get going. Take that chair.
C: (Takes hold of chair.) Where will I take it to?
S: I mean, take the chair and sit down.
C: (Sits on floor with chair on lap.)
S: I mean, sit on the chair.
C: (Finally sits on chair.)
S:: All right, here we go. (Puts head under cloth and
   motions up and down with his hand. Comedian
   thinks he should stand up, so he stands.) Say, what
   are you standing up for?
C: Didn't you motion with your hand for me to stand
   up?
S: No, you dumb cluck, I wanted you to raise your chin
   a little. Now get back on the chair. Comedian sits
   on chair and Straight puts head under cloth again.
C: (Starts across room again and picks up pin.)
S: (In exasperation) What are you doing?
C: I found a pin
S: Well,what of it? The point was towards me. What of
   that?
C: That's good luck. My mother told me when I find a pin
   with the point toward me to always pick it up. It's good
   luck.
S: You get back on that chair and stay there or you'll be
   in bad luck.
Comedian sits on chair and Straight puts head under cloth
again.
C: (Starts across room again and picks up another pin.)
S: What are you doing over there?
C: I just found another pin.
S: What of it?
C: The point was towards me.
S: What of that?
C: I picked it up. It's good luck.
S: You always pick up a pin when the point is toward you?
C: Yes. It's good luck.
S: Get back on that chair and stay there.

Comedian sits and Straight puts head under cloth. Comedian goes after another pin. Straight goes to chair and pretends to bend a pin and put it on the seat, point up.

S: Now what?

C: I just found another pin. The point was towards me. I picked it up. It's good luck.

S: You always pick up a pin when the point is towards you, don't you?

C: Sure. Its good luck.

S: Well, hurry and sit down.

C: (Sits down on supposed pin, screams, jumps up, and feels rear with hands.)

S: Now what are you screaming about?

C: I found another pin.

S: You did?

C: The point was towards me. I picked it up.

S: You should always pick up a pin when the point is toward you. It's good luck.

C: This one was bad luck.

S: Do you know something? There are over a billion pins manufactured in the U.S. every year, and no one knows where they all go to.

C: By golly, I know where that one went.

S: Now sit down and let me get this picture.

Comedian sits down, first feeling for a pin on chair. Straight puts head under cloth and pretends to make an exposure. Straight brings out funny face picture and gives it to Comedian.

C: What's this?

S: That's your picture.

C: That don't look like me.

S: That looks just like you.

C: Look at that eyes.

S: Just like your eyes.

C: Look at them nose.

S: Just like your nose.

C: And that mouths.

S: Looks just like your mouth. It's the most natural mouth I ever saw.
C: That don't look like me and I won't take it.
S: It looks just like you and you'll have to take it.
C: Well, I'll be gosh danged. If that looks like me, then this looks like you. (Turns over picture and shows donkey.)

VENTRILOQUIST ACT WITH SHORTY

Ventriloquist: Did you always live in the city?

Shorty: No. We used to live on a farm in Oklahoma. Dad was just a poor farmer. We had only one room in our house, and we had to eat and sleep all in one room.

V: Gee! You must have been awfully poor.

S: Yep, we was. But we got rich. A man came and dug a hole on dad's farm and struck oil and all at once, we was rich.

V: I bet that made you feel good.

S: Sure it did. And right away we moved to the city and got a house with a whole lot of rooms. There was one room where all we did was to sit around in.

V: That was the living room.

S: Is that what it was? Then there was another room where all we did was to eat in.

V: That was the dining room.

S: I guess so. Then, there was another room where all we did was to cook in.

V: That was the kitchen.

S: Then upstairs, there was a lot of rooms where all we did was to sleep in.

V: Those were the bedrooms.

S: And down at the end of the hall was a room all in white.

V: That was the bathroom.

S: Along the wall was a long white watering trough.

V: That was the bathtub.

S: Was it? Pa had it taken out. He said even if he did have some cattle, he couldn't get them upstairs to water them. Then there was a place to wash in.

V: That was a wash bowl or lavatory.

S: We didn't have no such fancy name for it. Then there was
   another little bowl with a lid. It really had two lids. One
   of them was all wore through and they put a new one on top
   of it. That was to wash our feet in. I could stand on one foot
   and put the other foot in and wash it, and when I wanted
   clean water, I pulled a chain. Pa didn't never wash his
   feet, and he had that taken out, too. He took the lid with
   the hole in it and framed Grandma's photograph, and he
   gave the good lid to Aunt Jennie to use for a bread board.
The act finishes with song sung by Shorty. Here is an example.

> I've travelled all over this country,
> I've stopped in the best of hotels.
> Some of the rooms were airy,
> Some of the rooms were like cells.
> Some of the cells had no windows,
> Some had not even a seat.
> And you all will sure die with laughter
> When I tell you what we had to eat.
>
> On Monday we had bread and gravy,
> On Tuesday had gravy and bread,
> On Wednesday had bread without gravy,
> On Thursday had plain bread instead.
> On Friday I went to the landord.
> "I am so hungry!" I said.
> So Saturday morning by way of a change
> We had gravy without any bread.

ON MAKING RAG PICTURES

Making rag pictures as is done by rag picture artists at vaudeville entertainments is not as difficult as might be imagined. Besides being beautiful and attractive, these pictures possess an apparent depth not easily obtained through the medium of crayon or brush and oil. To make a rag picture, follow these instructions and get surprising results.

The best material to use is canton flannel, because the fuzz on this material will cause the pieces of cloth to stick to each other without the aid of any special adhesive. Canton flannel (sometimes referred to as cotton flannel) can be purchased in several different colors, but when the desired color cannot be obtained, white flannel may be dyed the necessary shade by the use of household dyes or the well-known dye and tinting soaps. Other kinds of cloth may be used, but the double-faced canton flannel is best. Very small detail, like a line or stripe, may be put on the cloth with a brush and ink but as little as possible of this should be done.

A drawing board, a piece of wallboard, or several pieces of light board held together by cleats may be used as a support for the assembled pieces of cloth.

It is best to make an original picture, but if the aspirant does not possess the artist's talent necessary for this, postcards, art studies or sketches in magazines may be copied. Commence by making a small sketch, using colored crayon. Enlarge this to the desired size by hand, the pantograph or the well-known system of squares. Using this large sketch as a guide, cut the cloth of proper color into the correct size and shape, and assemble them on the supporting board. The first picture may be easily constructed by the aid of the following instructions and illustrations. The size of this sample picture will be 24 by 36 inches.

Obtain a piece of sky blue canton flannel, sized 18 by 36 inches. With a black crayon pencil or a pointed stick dipped in ink, draw a line across it at a distance of 13 and one half inches from its upper edge. This is to define the horizon as shown at X, Figure 1. Lay this on the supporting board, with its upper edge at the top of the board. Cut a piece of light green cloth according to the shape and size shown in Figure 2. Lay this on the supporting board with its lower edge at the bottom of the board. The two pieces will now have the appearance of Figure 3 and will form the sky, ocean, and foreground. The details of the picture are shown in the smaller illustrations. Make them according to the dimensions given and place them in position. From red material cut a semicircular piece and place it in position at the horizon line, as shown in the completed picture. This is the sun, Figure 4, which will require a reflection cut from cloth of a lighter shade of red, according to Figure 5. The rocks, Figure 6, are made out of brown or grey material and placed in position at the water's edge. Figure 7, the sandy spot on the left-hand bluff, is made out of light brown material. The cabin, Figure 8, may be made from brown and black striped material, which will give it a log effect. The windows and door are made of black cloth, and other detail may be put on with brush and ink. Cut the chimney and smoke according to fancy, and assemble all near the lower left hand corner. The path, Figure 9, is made from light brown material and may lead towards the tree or may be curved and lead to the seashore. The tree, Figure 10, is made from black material according to size and dimension. The completed picture is shown in Figure 13. The addition of foliage on the tree may be made by shaping a piece from dark green material, as in Figure 11, and placing it on the bare branches. A lighthouse, Figure 12, may be placed on the left bluff. Cut this from light material and paint on the windows and door. Additional detail such as pump, fence, wood pile, etc., may be added if desired.

If this picture is to be torn down and reassembled frequently for exhibition purposes, the adhesive quality of the fuzz or nap on the flannel must be used to hold the pieces to each other. If the picture is to be a permanent one, small dabs of glue may be used to hold the pieces in position. The picture looks best when viewed from a distance.

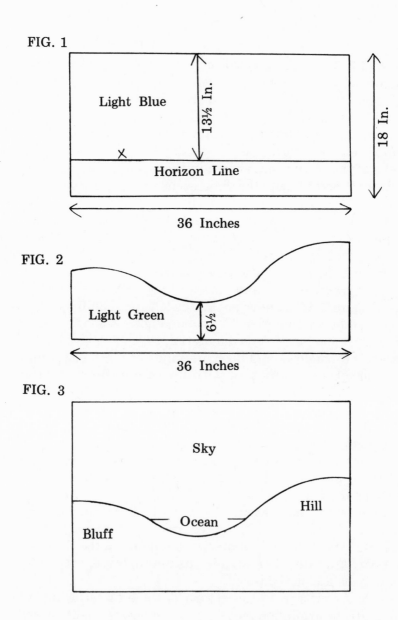

FIG. 1

Light Blue

13½ In.

× Horizon Line

18 In.

36 Inches

FIG. 2

Light Green

6½

36 Inches

FIG. 3

Sky

Hill

Bluff

Ocean

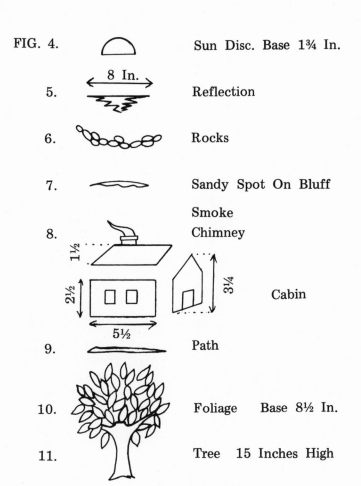

FIG. 4.   Sun Disc. Base 1¾ In.

5.   8 In.   Reflection

6.   Rocks

7.   Sandy Spot On Bluff

Smoke

8.   Chimney

1½   2½   3¼   Cabin

5½

9.   Path

10.   Foliage   Base 8½ In.

11.   Tree   15 Inches High

COMPLETED PICTURE

Fifty copies of
The Life and Times of
Augustus Rapp
The Small Town Showman
have been specially bound
and each copy numbered.

———————